Auto-bibliography

ALSO BY ROB DOYLE

Here are the Young Men
This is the Ritual
Threshold

Rob Doyle

Auto-biblio-graphy

Swift

SWIFT PRESS

First published in Great Britain by Swift Press 2021

1 3 5 7 9 10 8 6 4 2

Text designed and set in Minion by Tetragon, London
Printed and bound in Great Britain by CPI Group (UK) Ltd, Croydon, CR0 4YY

A CIP catalogue record for this book is available from the British Library

ISBN: 978-1-80075-052-4
eISBN: 978-1-80075-053-1

To Roisin,
and to my Berlin friends

The confused medley of meditations on art and literature in which he had indulged since his isolation, as a dam to bar the current of old memories, had been rudely swept away, and the onrushing, irresistible wave crashed into the present and future, submerging everything beneath the blanket of the past, filling his mind with an immensity of sorrow, on whose surface floated, like futile wreckage, absurd trifles and dull episodes of his life.

J.K. HUYSMANS

I even remember the colour of the Mexican sky during the two days it took me to read the novel.

ROBERTO BOLAÑO

CONTENTS

INTRODUCTION

In her book *The Writing Life*, Annie Dillard asks what it means to live a good life. 'There is no shortage of good days,' she writes. 'It is good lives that are hard to come by... Who would call a day spent reading a good day? But a life spent reading – that is a good life.'

There's something to this. Holding a characteristically gloomier view, Michel Houellebecq insists in his revering study *H.P. Lovecraft: Against the World, Against Life*, that 'Those who love life do not read. Nor do they go to the movies, actually. No matter what might be said, access to the artistic universe is more or less entirely the preserve of those who are a little fed up with the world.'

There's something to this too. In my case, reading has always served a dual purpose. In a positive sense, it offers sustenance, enlightenment, the bliss of fascination. In a negative sense, it is a means of withdrawal, of inhabiting a reality quarantined from one that often comes across as painful, alarming or downright distasteful. In the former sense, reading is like food; in the latter, it is like drugs or alcohol.

Throughout 2019, I contributed a weekly books column to the *Irish Times*. The premise was simple: every Saturday I would write about an old book of my choice. The newspaper's literary editor published the column with the alternating tag lines 'A year of Rob Doyle's best-loved books', and 'Rob Doyle's year of rereading'. The only rules were that I had to choose books written before the twenty-first century, and

I had to keep my articles to a word limit of 340. While the latter constraint was often frustrating, I viewed it as a stimulating formal challenge. Could I say something fresh and illuminating about a given book, or at least interestingly convey my enthusiasm, on such a modest canvas? Could I capture something of a book's essence, reflect a sliver of its tone and atmosphere, and not waste everyone's time by merely writing a glorified summary? Discussing a tome like *Moby-Dick* at such brevity bordered on the absurd, but the word count forced me to pare down my insights – more to the point, my passions – till they attained, I liked to think, the book-chat equivalent of haiku condensation.

I wrote the column while I was living in Berlin and on a hiatus from social media, so for much of the time I had no sense of what kind of response it was eliciting. In the autumn, I briefly returned to Dublin to give readings at book festivals. At these events, readers approached and told me they had been following my column. Some of them remarked on the relatively low proportion of fiction I selected, which they found surprising considering that that was the genre in which I had established myself as a writer. True enough, of the fifty-two entries, only twenty-three cover works of fiction – and even among these lie a number of generically contestable works (is Alexander Trocchi's *Cain's Book* fiction or memoir? Is Geoff Dyer's *But Beautiful* a book about jazz that employs fictive elements, or a fictional work that happens to tell us something about jazz? Is André Breton's *Nadja* really a novel? What about Clarice Lispector's *Água Viva*?).

While the project was conceived as a corralling of the books that shaped me as a writer and as a man, it also inevitably reflected my present interests as a reader, and I simply don't read as many novels as I used to. When I was in my twenties, novels were my staple, the primary means by which I understood the world and my place in it. Nowadays, novels are more like the dessert: the main course is large helpings of non-fiction, including criticism, philosophy, aphorisms, history and books about what the internet is doing to me. I have an unslakable thirst for autobiographical writing of all sorts, including diaries and letters. In general I have a predilection for novels that don't act like novels – the sort of generically slippy works mentioned above. Regardless of genre, I read for delight and fascination even when these sensations demand a toll, opening old wounds or inflicting new ones. The column is a record of sometimes masochistic enthusiasms.

The oldest work I discuss, the *Dhammapada*, dates back to the first century BC. Chronologically speaking I then skip to the second century AD (Marcus Aurelius), then on another couple of hundred years to the fifth century (Saint Augustine). I then take a running jump from the eighth to the seventeenth centuries (*The Tibetan Book of the Dead* to La Rochefoucauld), before landing at the commencement of modernity in the nineteenth century. The majority of the books I selected – forty-two of them – were written in the twentieth century, beginning in 1928 and streaking right to the millennial threshold. In fact, I cheated a little with Emmanuel Carrère's *The Adversary*, which was published in 2000 – I just really wanted to write about Carrére. I also cheated, slightly and for the same reason, with Roberto Bolaño's *Antwerp*, in that I dated it from the year when it was written (1980) rather than the year it was finally published (2002).

I dispute Martin Amis's assertion that we read even the classics in translation reluctantly. To me, reading a book from a familiar culture can feel like a drab sojourn in some rainy Dublin suburb, when I might travel instead to a far-off country. There are books here by authors from Russia and Asia, South America and North Africa, the United States and the United Kingdom, Germany and Switzerland, Hungary and Czechoslovakia, *fin-de-siècle* Austria and ancient Rome, along with a disproportionate number of books by French writers. The nationality most conspicuous by its absence is the Irish. This is not out of perversity or national self-abnegation on my part, but because, shortly before commencing the column, I had finished editing an anthology of Irish literature: as a reader I wanted to wander again – the more exotic the destination, the better.

Such a column would hold scant appeal, I think, if it were intended as an objective guide to literature, a canon-reinforcing round-up of the greatest works detached from any subjective experience, any life in reading. My intention was both more modest and more self-serving: the column would be about the books that formed me, sentimentally and intellectually, as well as the books that are *re*forming me now, and even the books that *de*formed me. I relished the project and wanted to take it further. And so, after the year ended and I moved temporarily back to Ireland, I began to expand it with memories and reflections on books, reading and writing, and the life through which they've flowed. As I was doing this, the world changed, suddenly and dramatically,

4

and so the book became about that too – a real-time bearing witness to a vast event whose ramifications, as I write this preface at the outset of a muted, cancelled summer, are indeterminable.

1 SVETLANA ALEXIEVICH

The Unwomanly Face of War (1985)

Translated by Richard Pevear and Larissa Volokhonsky

The Nobel Prize in Literature can be hard to take seriously, but we should be grateful to it for bringing to global attention the work of Svetlana Alexievich. Her first book is a wonder constructed on top of a simple, radical idea: 'Everything we know about war we know with "a man's voice"', but how might war appear when described in the voices of women who lived through it? How does killing feel to beings who generate new life from their own bodies?

In the 1970s and '80s, Alexievich travelled around the Soviet Union and spoke to women who had lived through – and fought in – the Second World War, recording their experiences on tape and in notebooks. Persisting against wary publishers and hostile censors, she fashioned from these amassed voices a literary form that carried the spiritual drama of great Russian literature into the twentieth century. While Dostoevsky and Tolstoy put the resources of the realist novel at the service of their visions, Alexievich arranges her chorus of voices into a work of non-fictional art. I defy any reader not to be continuously moved by pity, awe and horror as these stories come pouring forth, some lasting several pages, others in mere fragments.

'I think of suffering as the highest form of information,' writes Alexievich, before bringing us to the brink of information overload. In our volatile historical phase in which a third world war feels increasingly probable, *The Unwomanly Face of War* can be read as a primer for a descent into hell. The horror really is abyssal. Yet the strange, sobering revelation of the book lies in how tenderness and pity manifest alongside savagery on every page. The war that Alexievich presents is one of small, piercingly human moments salvaged from oblivion. It is a humbling read. At the outset of her career, Svetlana Alexievich established her mastery of a literary form as majestic, capacious and tragic as Russia itself.

In Cormac McCarthy's novel The Road, *while wandering a decimated earth in the aftermath of an unspecified holocaust, the nameless protagonist recalls standing in 'the charred ruins of a library where blackened books lay in pools of water. Shelves tipped over. Some rage at the lies arranged in their thousands row on row.' In our own (just about)* pre-apocalyptic world, *rather than be vandalised in fury at the false promise of meaning they embody, it seems likelier that libraries will gradually vanish from the surface of a connected and digital planet whereon they have come to seem anachronistic, no longer justifying the expense required to keep them open. I may be part of the last generation to whom the library was a place of formation, a resource and a sanctuary. When I was a child, my mother, who left school to work in her early teens, brought me and my brother to the local library, having internalised a radio presenter's maxim that there is no better gift you can give your child than the gift of reading. As a teenager I would return to the same library to borrow cassette albums (thus discovering The Smiths and Public Enemy) or order in books by Sylvia Plath and William Burroughs. A decade later, the libraries of north-east London provided me not only with stacks of books, but with a workspace. Living in a shared house near Finsbury Park – and when I say shared, I mean there were* nine *of us crammed into that semi-detached dump – it was not possible to write at home. The fact that one of my flatmates was an unemployed Bulgarian DJ who blared his skull-pounding trance from dawn till dusk was a factor. I wrote my first novel in Stamford*

Hill Library, cycling there daily with my laptop and a flask of coffee after I got home from work. Unemployed or homeless people likewise frequented the place, reading the newspapers or studying. I'm convinced that the blackness of that first novel of mine was in part a symptom of my Raskolnikovian pique at dwelling in that squalid house with those noisy Vulgarians – but how much blacker it would have been had I no library to go to! If books themselves are to disappear as physical objects, raptured up into the digital immanence, then rather than do away with libraries altogether, perhaps we ought to leave them standing, denuded of books but valued as sanctuaries of silence, honouring Nietzsche's contention that in a post-theistic epoch, churches should no longer hold a public-architectural monopoly on reflection and solitude.

2 ROBERTO BOLAÑO

Antwerp (1980)

Translated by Natasha Wimmer

Long before he attained world fame, the Chilean author
Roberto Bolaño wrote a very short novel that was so weird
he didn't even show it to any publishers. In a preface written
when *Antwerp* was finally published twenty-two years later,
Bolaño suggests the frazzled condition from which it had
emerged – 'My sickness, back then, was pride, rage and violence... I never slept' – before affirming the credo that makes
him such a seductive a figure to the young, the idealistic and
the damned: 'I believed in literature: or rather, I didn't believe
in arrivisme or opportunism or the whispering of sycophants.
I did believe in vain gestures, I did believe in fate.'

    Antwerp consists of fifty-six numbered and titled frag-
ments, which do not so much tell a story as hint at the existence of one that blew itself apart and left ghostly, radioactive
traces. Images recur: waiters silently traversing a windy beach;
deserted highways and hotels; 'cops who fuck nameless girls';
a hunchback in the woods. A writer, 'Roberto Bolaño', flickers
in an out of view, prey to hallucinations and disembodied
whispers. The effect is totally disorientating and incredibly
haunting. Bolaño throws his lot in with the core surrealist
technique of juxtaposing startlingly incongruous elements.
Narrative logic is shoved out of the speeding train. What
remains is a trance of pure atmosphere, the universe as
perceived by a shaman in the throes of delirium tremens.

In Bolaño's subsequent work the sensibility remained intact, but he came to his senses and began telling coherent stories, and they are very good. He always wrote, to use his own phrase, 'like a madman imitating a madman'. But *Antwerp* stands alone. It is a mysterious work, like a dream that confounds us on waking, suggesting depths beyond our knowable selves. It is also funny, like all Bolaño's work, even if the only 'joke' he cracks is a punchline that swallows its own tail: 'Remember that joke about the bullfighter who steps out into the ring and there's no bull, no ring, nothing?'

What is it we're reading for? I mean, why do we keep reading and rereading a particular novelist? When I think about Bolaño – and I think about him often – invariably I find my way to the conclusion that what I'm primarily in it for is friendship. That may sound corny, but there is no word that better conveys how I experience my relationship to his books. Admittedly it's a capacious, suggestive, not very literary-critical word. I could be more rigorous. I could say, for a start, that I love the way his mind works, its kinks and swerves and its boundless perversity; or, that I'm enthralled by his sense of humour as it manifests on every page in that uncommon fusion of mania and control, fanaticism and cool; or, that his novels and stories demonstrate to me a wholly different way of writing prose – looser and more intuitive, less rational or exact, wherein redundancy, commonplace, deadpan non-sequitur, metaphoric unspooling, erratic cliché and pretension are all tolerated within the broader poetical economy of a sentence – as if Bolaño were the culmination of an exotic tradition parallel to the Anglophone writing that otherwise shaped my sensibility, which of course he is. And all of that would be true. But the simpler truth is that I just like being around his books, in the same way that you cherish the company of a person you love, a friend.

3 FYODOR DOSTOEVSKY

Notes from Underground (1864)

Translated by Andrew R. MacAndrew

Is it preposterous to suggest that Fyodor Dostoevsky proph-
esied the election of Donald Trump, Brexit and the seething
hate-pits of social media? *Notes from Underground* is a vicious
slap in the face to the delusion that man is a rational being
who acts in his own self-interest. Dostoevsky's abject, cringing narrator, cowering in a basement hovel in St Petersburg,
insists that humankind would rather tear itself apart than
submit to boredom or obligatory happiness. The novel is a
scream of human perversity, and the most unflinching study
of self-loathing in the canon. As such, it is a vessel for painful
self-knowledge. Rereading it now, I see myself as I was at
twenty: odious, tortured, consumed by rage, obsessing over
perceived slights, compelled to act in incomprehensible
ways while veering between feelings of worthlessness and a
monstrous arrogance.

Notes from Underground pulled back the rock to uncover
a festering sub-layer of society whose existence literature
had hitherto failed to acknowledge. To Dostoevsky, such
tormented wretches as his underground man, who finger
their wounds until their thoughts grow sick and dangerous,
are the inevitable consequence of a liberalised society that
rejects tradition and religion, promising unlimited glory to
the individual only to subject him to humiliating material
conditions. Today's underground man is the high-school

shooter, the incel, Mohamed Atta, Anders Breivik, the online shamer, the self-hating troll. The underground man loathes everybody around him, because they are his mirrors. Like *Notes from Underground*, his days are an unrelenting ordeal of envy, spite, impotence, rancour, dissipation, vengefulness and shame.

As the novel opens, the narrator is forty – 'deep old age'. He is painfully sensitive, 'as if I'd had the skin peeled off me, so that contact with the very air hurts', and is still obsessing over humiliations he suffered when he was twenty-four. The only thing he has going for him is his lucidity, which is no comfort at all. He knows he is sick and hopes it gets worse, because after all, 'man adores suffering'.

Freud described a 'latency period' in sexual development, but there also exists – or there did in my case – a latency period in reading. For a gap of several years between a certain point in childhood and a certain point in adolescence, I didn't read a single book, fell entirely out of the habit. Previously, I'd been an avid reader. I look back on that early book-loving period as a state of innocence, a readerly Eden. As a child I read purely for pleasure; there was no effort, no sense of mission or obligation. I would become absorbed in a narrative, not impatiently projecting forward to what I might read next, nor taking notes, nor underlining, nor trying to remember. I read naively. And then I stopped reading, turning to other interests, namely video games and televised football. I played Doom *and* Command & Conquer *with the rapt concentration I had formerly trained on Roald Dahl's* The Witches, *Stephen King's* The Green Mile *series or* The Chronicles of Narnia. *Later, when I was about fifteen, I made a conscious decision to read again. From this point on, reading became a* project, *a campaign of simultaneous self-creation and self-destruction. I don't mean to suggest that I never again read for pleasure, only that the pure, unselfconscious absorption was lost. Post latency-period, I would read a book in part in order to have read it – not merely in a pretentious, status-conscious way, but in the sense that each book added a new tile to a never-to-be-completed mosaic of comprehension. Books became nodes in a network, existing in relation to one another – no longer the singularities of childhood reading, each book sufficient unto itself.*

4 MARGUERITE DURAS

Practicalities (1987)

Translated by Barbara Bray

When she was in her early seventies, the French novelist Marguerite Duras spoke to the writer Jérôme Beaujour about a range of subjects and memories that preoccupied her. Duras' musings were transcribed, she edited them, and the result is this consistently interesting book of miniature essays, autobiographical fragments and aphoristic reflections. Although Duras insists on the work's limitations – 'At most the book represents what I think sometimes, some days, about some things... The book has no beginning or end, and it hasn't got a middle either' – for my money it's at least as valuable as the fictions that ensured her renown. In a sense, it's a pity that authors must first prove themselves with the kinds of work – novels and short stories – that we consider the imprimatur of talent, before the publication of books like *Practicalities* becomes feasible. Relieved of the obligations of narrative and setting, such secondary works offer a more direct intimacy with an author's consciousness.

Practicalities might have been titled *Marguerite Duras Talks about Whatever Comes into Her Head*. The sections bear headings by turns prosaic and suggestive: 'The telly and death', 'Alcohol', 'Men', 'The pleasures of the 6th arrondissement', 'Hanoi', 'The smell of chemicals'. Duras reflects on her past work – such novels and films as *The Lover*, *Moderato cantabile* and *Hiroshima mon amour*. She writes bluntly about her alcoholism – 'What stops you killing yourself when you're intoxicated out of your mind is the thought that once you're dead you won't be able to drink any more' – and voices a provocative vision of the relations between men and women and the murky nature of sexual desire. She recounts a sexual encounter she had with an older boy when she was four years old, and another with a much older man on a train to Paris when she was a teenager, while her family were sleeping next to them. While the musings are personal rather than abstract, *Practicalities* hints at a broader truth: after the youthful romance of creative expression fades, writing is a vocation that makes no easy accommodation with happiness.

When I lived next to the Parc des Buttes-Chaumont in the nineteenth arrondissement of Paris, I used to go running in the mornings up and down the park's looping slopes. One day while walking home after my run, I got talking to a man who was sitting on the terrace of a café near my flat. He told me he came there every week. He drank pastis, conversed with the other old-timers who showed up, exchanged neighbourhood news or memories. He told me a story about how he had served in the navy back in the 1950s, and was present at France's first hydrogen bomb test. From the deck of one of the ships that ringed the test site somewhere in the Pacific, he had watched the mushroom cloud expand across the ocean sky. He showed me a faded photograph of himself as a young man, handsome in a white uniform, on his hunkers with two or three grinning seamen. That photograph was taken on the morning of the test, he told me, and all those men died in the years afterwards. At least, I think he showed me such a photograph. After our conversation, I never saw him again but I used what he'd told me as the basis for a short story. I wrote in the voice of an old, sentimental man who reflects on the brutal and historic experiences he underwent in his youth, memories that mingle with erotic reminiscences of his young wife who has long since died (reminiscences that were nourished by my own desire for a distant woman). In the story, after the hydrogen bomb test, the man goes to fight in the Algerian war, following orders and committing terrible acts. Again, I can't remember if the old man really did tell me he fought in that war. The fiction has become inextricably mixed with the testimony of which it was an imaginatively enhanced expression. It doesn't matter. I worked on that story for quite a while, but it never felt entirely right and I didn't publish it.

5 ARTHUR SCHOPENHAUER

Essays and Aphorisms (1851)

Translated by R.J. Hollingdale

In the history of ideas, the name Arthur Schopenhauer is indelibly linked with philosophical pessimism. True enough, Schopenhauer's vision of existence is unflinchingly tragic: 'For the world is Hell, and men are on the one hand the tormented souls and on the other the devils in it.' And yet, his synthesis of Western philosophy with Hindu and Buddhist metaphysics offers not only ethical guidance, but even solace and the possibility of redemption. Rereading him after a decade, I realised that such essays as 'On the Indestructibility of Our Essential Being by Death' had helped dissuade my younger self from nurturing an excessive fear of dying.

Schopenhauer despised writers who conceal shallow minds behind a veil of unintelligible language: if a writer is profound, he will seek the clearest possible expression of his ideas. The proof is in the prose: Schopenhauer's limpid thoughts are a pleasure to read even for those lacking formal philosophical training. As with all true philosophers, his starting point is appalled astonishment at that elephant in every conceivable room, 'the problem of existence' itself. Schopenhauer argued that behind the world of appearances lies a unified reality which he calls 'will'. The painful realm in which we fleetingly find ourselves alive is the ceaseless tumult of this blind and insatiable will. Desire is unsatisfiable, the essence of life is suffering, and the sole hope of redemption lies in ascetic negation of the will to live. Try to be patient and charitable towards your fellow human beings, because they are prisoners just like you are in the 'penal colony' of the universe.

Nightmare metaphysics aside, there are misanthropic observations on psychology, religion, aesthetics and writing. Take this aperçu, as relevant in today's book review pages as it was in nineteenth-century Germany: 'The art of *not* reading is a very important one. It consists in not taking an interest in whatever may be engaging the attention of the general public at any particular time... A precondition for reading good books is not reading bad ones: for life is short.'

Schopenhauer is right, the art of not reading is of the utmost importance. I am tempted here to list the books I have especially enjoyed not reading lately, a gleeful and bitter list full of names I hope are forgotten long before mine is, though I know they won't be. Every week I don't read new authors, and my pile of books not to be read grows higher by the day. I scour the books pages and literary websites for hints on which authors not to read next, and have even thought about setting up a rival website to Goodreads, called Notreads, where users can rate the books they haven't been reading. Sometimes it gets too much and I feel crushed by a desire not to read every book that's ever been written. And that's when it dawns on me that to some out there, it's my *books they look forward to not reading,* my *books they disdain as publicity-salted junk. Feeling chastened, sheepish, I make like Schopenhauer and turn for solace to the enigmas of the Pāli Canon:*

> *If you believe 'I am better than him', you are deluded.*
> *If you believe 'I am worse than him', you are deluded.*
> *If you believe 'I am neither better nor worse than him', you are deluded.*
> *If you believe 'I am his equal', you are also deluded.*

6 VIRGINIA WOOLF

A Room of One's Own (1929)

Virginia Woolf's attempt to answer the question of why literary history boasts so few female geniuses is celebrated as a feminist text, but less often remarked upon are its ingenuities of form and style. A narrative essay in which Woolf makes use of 'all the liberties and licences of a novelist', *A Room of One's Own* dramatises the thought processes that led the author to her conclusions ('Yet it seemed absurd, I thought, turning over the evening paper, that a man with all this power should be angry.').

And what conclusions are those? First and foremost, that the key factor holding women back was poverty: 'a woman must have money and a room of her own if she is to write fiction'. Woolf's argument concerns wealth and class as well as gender. (Idea for a polemic relating Dublin's housing crisis to the impoverishment of its intellectual culture: *A Gaff of One's Own*.) She enjoins women writers 'by hook or by crook' to get their hands on 'money enough to travel and to idle, to contemplate the future or the past of the world, to dream over books and loiter at street corners and let the line of thought dip deep into the stream'.

To Woolf, great poetry flows from minds unimpeded by anger or bitterness: 'incandescence' is the signal property of artistic flourishing. Works that betray their author's personal grudges – the 'desire to protest, to preach, to proclaim an injury, to pay off a score' – are doomed to a fatal sterility. And

27

so, paradoxically, women writers (widening the polemic, we might include working-class writers, gay writers, and so on) can incandesce only when they transcend their self-conscious identity as women writers – and money helps.

The beauty of *A Room of One's Own* is that it exemplifies the serenity of mind that Woolf insists is the defining quality of all great artists, whatever their gender. Her limpid and graceful essay is not only about securing the material conditions required to write in peace – it's also about self-overcoming.

'We all have the bookshops we deserve, except for those of us who have none,' writes Roberto Bolaño. We could each draw up an autobiographical atlas of the key bookshops of our lives – a list that would perhaps correspond to periods of erotic happiness. In Stoke Newington, London, there is a street called Church Street which I remember as being one of the most attractive places in the city at weekends. On that street there is a second-hand bookshop – or there used to be; it may be gone now. I used to visit on Saturdays or Sundays when I lived nearby, often while hung-over, often guilty or euphoric. The shop was run by a guy with white hair who always played jazz or classical. He seldom looked up from whatever paper he was reading or expressed judgement on what his customers bought. One exception: he became animated when I placed on his counter a proof copy of Reality Hunger: A Manifesto by David Shields, which had yet to be published. That book excited him, and when I read it, it excited me too. I generally bought second-hand books in those days because it was what I could afford. Which is not to say that when I visited the multi-storey Foyles on Charing Cross Road in the heart of the city I tended to come away empty-handed. That is where I went to meet my friend Andy after we finished work. We would roam the shop for hours, pausing at shelves to disparage some author or praise another. We both aspired to be writers, so the enormous bookshop appeared to us as a citadel to be stormed. The curious thing is that I ought to be staying in a bookshop right now. As I write this page we are in the midst of what has just been declared a pandemic. The world is shutting down. We are all confined within our own borders, our own homes, our own skulls. It's springtime and I'm alone in a house in Rosslare Harbour, up a steep hill from the beach. Last Friday, my girlfriend and I were meant to walk down the steps to the port and board a ferry that would take us overnight to Cherbourg in Normandy. From Cherbourg we would take a train to Paris, and there spend a few nights at the flat above the Shakespeare and Company bookshop in the Latin Quarter, which looks out on the Seine and the Notre Dame cathedral (or its blackened shell). Of course, the trip was cancelled, as the entirety of normal life has been cancelled. What this event means – if it's the start of an endless falling, or will clear the way for a better world, or a world that's the same but drearier – it's impossible to know. For now, there is disquiet, and amazement verging on dark euphoria.

7 ARTHUR KOESTLER

The Gladiators (1939)

Translated by Edith Simon

The life Arthur Koestler recounts in his two amazing volumes of autobiography, *The Invisible Writing* and *Arrow in the Blue*, is as full of adventure and suspense as that of James Bond, if only James Bond were a brilliant intellectual and a member of the Communist Party who took breaks from writing books to fight in the Spanish Civil War. Koestler eventually lost faith in Communism, and his superb first novel, *The Gladiators*, is a dramatisation of that apostasy, though it concerns the slave revolt of Spartacus rather than the Bolshevik Revolution. The first book in a trilogy exploring the question of whether the revolutionary end justifies the means – *Arrival and Departure* and *Darkness at Noon* are no less great – it is full of everything one wants from a historical novel. When I read it, it astonished me that a story so dramatic and rich with mythic resonance could really have happened.

In fact, the historical record of the slave uprising is rather slim: with gusto Koestler does what any novelist should, filling in the blanks with vividly imagined scenarios. After leading seventy fellow gladiators to fight their way out of captivity, Spartacus is hailed as the slave messiah. He directs his bid for emancipation from inside the crater of Mount Vesuvius. Every hero risks becoming a tyrant: Spartacus is faced with terrible choices, and the revolution loses direction. The novel ends with an unforgettable scene of retributive mass crucifixion, the road to Rome lined with the groaning bodies of rebels.

Although Koestler wrote *The Gladiators* in part to examine the nature of revolutionary failure and explore his disappointment in the lost utopian dream of Communism, as with all good allegorical novels the story stands up on its own. Koestler wrote it in German, having written previously in Hungarian. He would go on to write many more books in English – in prose that is at least the match of most native stylists.

*A university education irrevocably changes the way we read.
Growing accustomed to scouring for information, assimilating
concepts and constructing from these materials a superstructure
of thought that transcends a given text (there's another thing
that changes during college: beforehand we'd never refer to a
book as a 'text'), we become, by one definition, intellectuals:
people who read with pens in their hands. Ever since college I've
used a pen the way American teenagers use Ritalin – to focus.
A pen anchors me in choppy prosaic seas, gives me a point on
which to fix my constantly scattering attention. After I grad-
uated, giddy at a sudden freedom from structured reading,
I wanted to binge on novels. However, after years of scrutinising
dense philosophical texts, I found I didn't quite know what to
do with myself while reading fiction. You couldn't really profit
from reading novels with a pen in your hand. I needed to
recalibrate my brain so that it didn't merely scan for concepts
and blocks of assimilable information, but became receptive
again to the subtler qualities of fiction. Once you leave home
you can never truly return, however, and I never fully regained
my ability to be engrossed in pure story. If all that's going on
is yarn-spinning, with narrative proffered as an end in itself,
I'll sit there thinking, 'What's the point of this?' Incidents,
setting, character – these are well and good, but if there are
no ideas charging through them I get restless. This explains
why a certain strain of high-information fiction became my
drug of choice – the kind of novel with as much essay in it
as narrative, the kind you can read with a pen in your hand*

(Michel Houellebecq's novels, for instance). Anyway, I must have gotten over the worst of my post-college awkwardness about reading fiction, because I spent the next couple of years imbibing the stuff pretty indiscriminately, plucking titles from the book-swap shelves at hostels and cafés in Luang Prabang or Phnom Penh, Sucre or Cuzco. There was a quality of enforced and salutary randomness to this kind of reading. Books were selected not according to literary fashion or online hype (social media was still in its infancy); you read whatever you could find that looked sufficiently interesting, paperbacks that had been left behind by some other wanderer. Reading thus became generatively unsystematic again.

8 FRIEDRICH NIETZSCHE

On the Genealogy of Morals (1887)

Translated by Walter Kaufmann

One way to think of *On the Genealogy of Morals* is as among the greatest horror novels ever written. Ostensibly a work of philosophical anthropology, its content is so speculative and shocking that it has more in common with Lovecraft than with Kant.

The nature of Nietzsche's mission was staggering: cosmic regime change, a blasting of humankind out of its Judaeo-Christian echo chamber. God was dead, but the assumptions embedded in religious belief ran deep into the foundations of our civilisation, beneath the cheery parades of supposed atheism. Every theistic prejudice would eventually be uprooted, even if it took millennia, and thus we were now 'part of a higher history than all history hitherto'. As Nietzsche remarked with breathtaking offhandedness in one of his letters, the first thing that will have to go is our entire European morality.

Genealogy is Nietzsche's bid to trigger moral Armageddon. In three seditious essays, he argues that everything Christians believe to be good was born of seething *ressentiment*, the hatred of slaves for the sanguinity of their noble Roman masters. Christianity was a conspiracy of the weak, ugly and vengeful to effect a 'slave revolution in morals' and cast shame on everything that had previously been called good: lust, power, riches, freedom of spirit. Christian 'love' was spawned from infinite hate, a spitefulness that forced the world to assume its own mangled image. Life became poisoned by guilt. Moreover, the democrats and socialists who agitate for the equality of all human beings are Christians in drag: they boast of having done away with God, but assume they can somehow hang on to the morality His reign ensured.

Nietzsche still reads like the most urgent headline news. He knew full well that one day, great cataclysms would be associated with his name. From *Genealogy* onwards, the battle lines were drawn. Nietzsche committed himself to total war, accepted his adversarial destiny, opened negotiations with Evil. This book could only have been written by the Antichrist.

I once wrote a semi-autobiographical story about a writer who attempts to write a book about Nietzsche as his life implodes. In the story, the narrator's girlfriend is Russian; in reality, she was Vietnamese. The story ends with the woman leaving the narrator, though when I wrote it my then girlfriend and I were still living together in the same dusty Hampstead flat where the story is set – all of which would confirm my nascent intuition that much fiction is anticipated fact. In the story, the narrator longs to visit Turin, the city where Nietzsche spent his final years of sanity. But he never gets there, and in the end he abandons hope of writing a book. A couple of years after the story was published, I did travel to Turin, in the company of the woman who had translated the story into French. On arriving in the city we located the Piazza San Carlo, where Nietzsche is said to have fallen to his knees and embraced a horse that was being whipped, his hold on sanity lost thereafter. Just off the square was a bronze bust which made Nietzsche look even more stern and militaristic than usual. A blustery text hailed the 'philosopher of power' and – absurdly – trumpeted Italian patriotism: the plaque had been instated by Mussolini, to recruit the bellicose German to his chauvinist cause. In those days, I still imagined I might one day write a book about Nietzsche, succeeding where the character in my short story had failed. I know now it will never happen. The moment has passed. As we age, our relationship to the work of authors we once revered evolves. There is a diminution of intensity, hence of fascination. When I first started reading Nietzsche, I was young and he was old – older than me anyway, old enough to seem an unimpeachable authority, cloaked in world-historic glamour. A couple of years ago, I passed the age Nietzsche was when he wrote Human, All Too Human. Soon I'll enter the stage of life he was at when he wrote his genius works, the books that upended my entire vision of life when I was in my twenties. No one who is younger than we are ever seems like an unassailable authority. I relate to Nietzsche now as a strange and brilliant man who was limited in certain respects, myopic and dangerously mistaken in others. This is what it means to mature, to inhabit the high noon of life: authorities and doctrines fall away. There is nothing left to be converted to. You find yourself standing – in a Nietzschean sort of way – at a serene peak of understanding, surveying the lowlands and hills you passed to get to where you are now, a landscape strewn with the husks of selves you discarded en route. From here on in there are no longer any guides, no charts other than the ones you yourself draw up.

9   JEAN BAUDRILLARD

America (1986)

Translated by Chris Turner

Everybody knows that the best philosophers write like novelists and the best novelists write like philosophers. Jean Baudrillard wrote at the event horizon where postmodern theory and science fiction become indistinguishable. Fittingly, the Wachowskis even asked him to appear in a sequel to *The Matrix*. Baudrillard declined, claiming that *The Matrix* was exactly the kind of film the Matrix would make about the Matrix.

According to Baudrillard, the real has vanished into images of itself: we are now in the age of the simulation. There is an unapologetic nihilism in his post-Marxist evocations of a 'cool' world wherein all values have been flattened out, a universe without depth where glinting surfaces reflect each other and every human gesture is a stylised simulacrum.

America is the French provocateur's road trip across a New World whose banality and strangeness fascinate him. On the freeways, malls, deserts and cities of the USA, he discerns an ecstatic vacuity, an apotheosis of the hyperreal. For Baudrillard, the desert is the ultimate metaphor for America – empty, vast, radiant, indifferent, sublime. And like everything else, the desert has been absorbed into cinema: we cannot gaze at its horizon without seeing through the lens of John Ford, perceiving strata of astral mythology.

Baudrillard is a maestro of that peculiarly French kind of sentence which doesn't necessarily mean anything, but drips with poetic suggestion. *America* consists largely of observations such as this: 'Here in the transversality of the desert and the irony of geology, the transpolitical finds its generic, mental space.' The cumulative effect is mesmeric, and the insights are often haunting: 'There is nothing more mysterious than a TV set left on in an empty room… It is as if another planet is communicating with you.' To Baudrillard, the ubiquitous American smile 'signifies only the need to smile. It is a bit like the Cheshire Cat's grin: it continues to float on faces long after all emotion has disappeared.'

Today, the America we thought we knew has vanished. Baudrillard suggests it was never really there.

On the day of the September 11, 2001 attacks I was working in my bullshit job, which involved – no joke – separating supermarket coupons into discrete piles, in a building on an industrial estate in Dublin seemingly devoted to this mindless activity. That job separating coupons is one of quite a few dismal jobs I worked at in those years, wasting the precious time of my youth, the time of my life. I bitterly regret all that wasted time now but I regretted it even more then. I don't know why I let myself do it. I do know why: for the money, and because I grew up in a proletarian culture in which wasting your youth at menial jobs was the done thing. I worked at part-time jobs during my last couple of years of school, and at one particularly wretched job throughout college. Of the many things I regret there are few I regret more than working through college, when college ought to be a time for the free play of the mind and senses, a time of idle curiosity, of languorous afternoons spent discussing Virginia Woolf or Dadaism with beautiful girls. None of that for me. I was working at a tedious job and, looking back, my employment exacerbated the severely unbalanced, indeed tortured relationship I had with time in those years. Live without dead time, *ran a slogan by the Situationists, a movement which interested me as a rancorous young pseudo-Marxist. It was meant as an exhortation to relish one's time but for me it had the effect of rendering time an affliction, making me acutely aware of each passing second I was wasting at work and not spending at more fulfilling activities. I would swing from boredom and frustration during shifts, to a crazed*

41

determination to relish my time whenever I was hoping to enjoy myself. My desire to enjoy myself was so acute that enjoyment was impossible. We don't say, in such instances, 'I got pleasantly tipsy,' we say, 'I got hammered.' We don't say, 'Let's smoke a joint,' we say, 'Let's get fucking blitzed.' One definition of having a good time is being immersed in whatever it is you're doing, but my ability to immerse myself in anything other than my neurosis was strangled by a painful awareness of time and how much or little of it I had left. It got so bad that whenever I went to hang out with friends, I had to ask them to cover up any visible clocks, including the LCD faces on stereos or DVD players. I knew it must have seemed like an affectation but it was impossible for me to unwind when time was winding me up, staring me down, psyching me out. The injunction to live without dead time became so entrenched that after I left college, the dynamic of clock-watching and putting the hours in established itself in inverted form. Not working became my full-time job. A good day was one in which I did nothing I didn't want to do, no matter how futile or empty the day otherwise was. I had saved up quite a bit of money working through college, and I used it to drift around Asia and Latin America for a couple of years. Being in those places, whose weaker economies meant I could get by on very little, became an end in itself, a form of negative accomplishment. For two and a half years I gained a sense of achievement from doing nothing. That stage of life – early to mid-twenties – is when most young people are out establishing themselves in a career, and in a way I was doing just that, serving an apprenticeship in idleness – which in some sense has culminated in my life as a writer.

But Beautiful (1991)

With this sequence of portraits of famous jazz musicians, Geoff Dyer commenced a streak of dauntingly good books that calls to mind Maradona's run to score against England in the 1986 World Cup: no matter how often you watch, you're not quite sure how he pulled it off. Unlike Maradona, Dyer is a working-class son of Gloucestershire, but he speaks fluent American, and this is the work of a man in love – with jazz and the whole national mythoscape behind it.

But Beautiful is criticism in the form of fiction, though it's not really criticism so much as rhapsodic evangelism – which is the best kind of criticism. In a long afterword, Dyer quotes George Steiner – 'The best readings of art are art' (a phrase which has two pertinent meanings here) – and insists that 'all art is also criticism'. Whether he knew it or not, Dyer was thus setting the terms for the body of work he has been unfurling ever since, which effects a complete dissolution of the boundary between commentary and artwork, as in a mystical experience wherein subject and object merge. Incidentally, *But Beautiful* is strong proof of the exquisitely sensitising effects of cannabis, which Dyer has claimed was indispensable to the book's creation.

The prose is dulcet and superfine, soloing rapturously alongside the music it invokes. It makes for brilliant portraiture: Lester Young as fragile as porcelain, 'landlocked in the middle of a century'; Charles Mingus the juggernaut;

Thelonious Monk the man-baby; Chet Baker; Duke Ellington; Bud Powell; Art Pepper; Ben Webster. These were damaged and neurotic men, often addicted to alcohol or heroin, blowing the blues of being black in unformed America. Playing like a man possessed, Dyer keeps hitting the sweet spot of critical insight: Monk 'played each note as though astonished by the previous one'; Young's sound 'was soft and lazy but there was always an edge in it somewhere.' Crucially, *But Beautiful* passes the acid test for any work of this kind. It makes you thirst for the music.

'Wanting to meet a writer because you like his work is like wanting to meet a duck because you like pâté.' So Margaret Atwood reminds us, and she is right in almost every case, the exception being my friendship with Geoff Dyer, which followed so naturally from my long-standing enthusiasm for his books that it felt like the next chapter, a psychedelic extension of his writing into an extra-literary space which is the writing's apotheosis, in that it dissolves the border separating art and life and thus fulfils the utopian promise conjured across Dyer's work. Usually I can admire a writer's books very much yet have no desire to enjoy a friendship with them beyond the metaphysical friendship that literature facilitates (that literature is). In Geoff's case it was different in that, from virtually the moment I first read his work – was first cracked up by it – I felt the stirrings of an impulse to make this person know about me, to somehow become part of his life and invite him into my own. Which really does sound incredibly stalkerish, and so acting as my own defence attorney let me point out that in these matters I tend to be exceedingly and even excessively reserved, reckoning it better not to impose on people. But I eventually did crowbar my way into Geoff Dyer's life, and when, a couple of years ago, he came to stay in Berlin for the summer and we hung out daily, it was on one hand an extraordinary delight – a 'peak experience', to use one of his preferred phrases – and on the other, as I said, perfectly natural, inevitable even. One year you were there reading and rereading Dyer's books about ecstatic drift, the narcotic sublime, transcendent idleness, and the next there was

Geoff in your flat in Friedrichshain on a Saturday night, waiting patiently (and neurotically) for you to portion out drugs to stuff in your underwear and smuggle into Berghain. He came back to Berlin the following summer, along with his wife Rebecca. This time my friends and I brought him not to Berghain but to the superior KitKatClub for what was, if I may say so myself, one of the all-time, MDMA-enhanced great nights, orchestrated to absolute perfection by me. My friend Andy was there too, having at the Christlike age of thirty-three his first ever drug experience (the guy has never even tasted alcohol or smoked a cigarette), raised to such jubilation that he really did seem Christlike for the night, wandering saucer-eyed and beatific among the lingerie-adorned bodies by the pool where the jazz band played. Geoff still texts me about that night, in tones of gratitude and wonderment, which just goes to show that the tables have turned. As I like to remind him, the big deal used to be that Geoff Dyer was coming to town, but now I prefer to think of his Berlin trips as Geoff's annual pilgrimage to the city where Rob Doyle lives.

11 *The Tibetan Book of the Dead*
   (eighth century A D)

Translated by Gyurme Dorje

Where should we turn when confronting the question of what
it means to die: to our own culture, which encourages denial
and panic, or to a culture such as that of Buddhist Tibet, in
which life was a long and careful preparation for death? The
high priests of scientific materialism assure us that all talk of
consciousness continuing after physical death is for children,
but the troubling visions presented in *The Tibetan Book of the
Dead* make annihilation seem like the fairy tale.

As with all great religious and spiritual texts, there is comfort in the reminder that the trials and agonies we face now
are not ours alone: human beings have been screwing things
up and suffering the consequences since time immemorial.
There is an element of existential slapstick to the section
titled 'Plaintive Confession of Rampant Egohood', as well
as gorgeous and visceral poetry: 'From beginningless time,
without end, I have roamed through cyclic existence... The
fires of blazing hatred have unabatingly seared my mind.'

Since its introduction to the West a century ago, *The
Tibetan Book of the Dead* (also known as the *Bardo Thodol*)
has spun a web of inspiration. Carl Jung was mesmerised by
it; first-wave psychedelic gurus like Timothy Leary admired
its awesome luminescence. The minimalist composer Éliane
Radigue produced her intense *Trilogie de la Mort* under its
influence, while the filmmaker Gaspar Noé's masterpiece

47

Enter the Void visualises its schema above a sleaze-scape of modern Tokyo.

The book includes strange prayers, masked dramas and references to bizarre local customs ('the semen should be inhaled through the nose, while it is still warm'). It is the section titled 'The Great Liberation by Hearing', though, that has done most to kindle the passions of a spiritually barren West. Intended to be read at the bedside of the dying, it describes the terrifying 'bardos' through which consciousness passes on being separated from the body. If we are sufficiently alert, we might seize the chance to escape the wheel of becoming. For the rest of us, 'The cycle of ignorance and bewilderment is exhausting and undiminishing.'

I bought my copy of The Tibetan Book of the Dead *in a shop called the Kali Psychedelic Bookshop, just off Boxhagener Platz in the Berlin neighbourhood of Friedrichshain. A bright and pleasant space, it was staffed by that earth-spanning tribe of preternaturally gorgeous psychedelic kids with whom I've always felt an affinity. In addition to shelves stacked with psychedelic and mystical literature, the store served a variety of teas which readers could sip while lounging on beanbags and cushions – like a backpackers' cafe in Laos or Cambodia. The scent of incense was perpetual. In the afternoons I would hang out there to read and listen in on the neo-hippies' keen, hushed conversations. I vaguely hoped they would invite me into their circle; I wanted to tell them I was a minor authority on the subject of psychedelics, had written about it and survived more terrifying trips than they'd had bong hits. But I didn't; we just smiled politely at each other and I turned back to my book. I felt that the place was good for the neighbourhood: psychedelic kids never harm anyone, and their thoughtful vibe and glow of vegan health offset Berlin's prevailingly scuzzy, confrontational aesthetic. After a few visits, it dawned on me that they were holding psychedelic drug sessions on the premises – that's what the hushed conversations were about. Small groups would vanish out the back, perhaps to smoke DMT, or would congregate with intent as the staff closed up shop – when the shutters came down, they were blasting off into the multiverse. For a few weeks I fell out of the habit of visiting the bookstore. One afternoon I returned in the hope of buying another book I needed for my newspaper column. There was no motion inside the premises, no sign by the door. I checked Google Maps, wondering if I was on the wrong street.* Permanently Closed, *it said in red text on my screen. And I thought: drug bust.*

12 PHILIP K. DICK

Valis (1981)

Imagine you woke up one morning and found everything was as it seemed. A reality TV star controlled the world's largest nuclear arsenal. Life on earth was presided over by omniscient tech corporations whose ambitions rivalled that of God. Citizens hooked on licit and illicit drugs shared their every thought in a global contest for followers and likes, and chose their sexual partners via handheld devices. Meanwhile, economic, political and meteorological systems were all winding down. Everything felt tacky and eschatological at once.

That's right, the first decades of the twenty-first century were written by a troubled science fiction novelist who died in 1982. Philip K. Dick has won the admiration of writers beyond his genre, including Roberto Bolaño, Martin Amis and Emmanuel Carrére (who wrote a biography titled *I Am Alive and You Are Dead*). I myself can no longer read his novels, the part of my brain that could follow twisty SF plots having long since burned out. However, there was a time when PKD's work invaded my dreams, in which shards of my exploded psyche pursued one another across looping timelines and unstable dimensions.

Working in a 1960s West Coast milieu of countercultural paranoia and political unrest, Dick churned out novels while caning a steady intake of amphetamine. In his final decade, he appears to have gone insane. Obsessed with a shattering metaphysical revelation, he wrote a massive 'Exegesis' detailing a rogue gnostic theology. One of his final novels, *Valis* presents itself as a fictional treatment of this cosmological meltdown. Its protagonist, Horselover Fat, stands in for Dick himself – or perhaps not, seeing as the narrator is named Phil, writes sci-fi novels and shares Horselover's concern that the Roman Empire never ended and we are trapped in a holographic 'Black Iron Prison'.

Philip K. Dick's disintegrating universe is bleak and psychotic, but perhaps we should think twice before attempting to escape. As Dick once warned: 'If you find this world bad, you should see some of the others.'

My girlfriend Roisin, who is the smartest person I know and who I often imagine marrying, has talked about getting a PKD-related tattoo: the insignia from Ubik, *Dick's novel of psychotic ontology that she regards as prophetic (and I regard as unreadable). Before we lived together in Berlin she got the eighth in the series of toe tattoos through which she is figuratively narrating her passage through life: every year or two, a new image on another toe, representing a key value or stage of personal evolution. If her toe tattoos are a book that tells the story of her life, it's a book I'm in the process of plagiarising, not in content but in form. In Germany I got the first in my own series of toe tattoos: a spiral on my right big toe, symbol of transcending the loops of habit and suffering, symbol too of a mystical something or other. Curiously, I don't think I will regret it. People who don't have tattoos often ask those who do whether they might not come to regret it, and generally speaking the answer ought to be: of course I will! Part of the point of getting a tattoo is that you'll regret it. Of course you'll regret a tattoo because of course you'll change, evolve, reassess your priorities as the cells in your body die away to be replaced by new ones. The person who got the tattoo is a version of you that you'll outlive, and it's this forever disappearing person that the tattoo honours. And that person knows it. That person is saying, 'Record a message from me now, before I change, before I change into you.' Not that he dislikes you, he just knows you're different. People talk about the permanence of tattoos but getting a tattoo is a tribute to transience. We get* tattoos in the same spirit in which we write books. The crucial thing in both cases is to do it while you still have the nerve to say what's true before it gets overlaid by other truths. Write books full of insight you know will vanish, that you know you'll come to regret voicing even, before you become someone else, someone mellower or happier, more compromised or timid, someone who can no longer withstand the truths you have it in you now to express. Even if you eventually regard such truths as dangerous mistakes, they'll have been your stepping stones to the knowledge of the future. Books and tattoos must be records of disappearing ideals. Years ago in Sarnath, the village outside Varanasi where the Buddha gave his first public discourse after attaining enlightenment, I met a conceptual artist from California who had many tattoos. Each bore a specific meaning that related to one of her artworks. The tattoo that stands out in my memory was a neat dark strip, a centimetre or so in breadth, which traced a line around the contours and planes of her body. If laid out flat, she told me, the line would measure one hundred metres. When I asked her the classic question – whether she might regret it – she smiled and gave an answer that stayed with me: 'The body doesn't last very long.'

13 JEAN RHYS

Quartet (1928)

The special misery of being alone, obscure and impecunious in a foreign city hangs thick over Jean Rhys's early fiction. Her protagonists are young or not-so-young women on the margins of bohemia in Paris or London, drifting from one dim bar to the next, a demi-monde inhabited by 'the Freaks who would never do anything' and 'the Freaks who just possibly might'.

Rhys's first novel *Quartet* employs a simpler, more naive style than the staccato modernese she developed through the 1930s, culminating in the Parisian dissolution of *Good Morning, Midnight*. Likewise set in Paris, *Quartet* presents in tight compaction the concerns that justify Rhys's place on the outsider fiction bookshelf: cynical sexual transaction; dejection and dependency amid smoky cafés and seedy hotels frequented by 'internationalists who invariably got into trouble sooner or later'.

Marya Zelli finds herself at the mercy of strangers when her Polish husband with whom she moved from London to Paris is imprisoned for theft. Dissipating what's left of her innocence, she is taken in by the Heidlers, a faintly sinister couple who are prominent in the expatriate art scene. Everybody fucks everybody else around, and everybody gets hurt.

Even through Marya's bleary eyes, Paris retains its seductive promise: 'From the balcony Marya could see one side of the Place Blanche. Opposite, the Rue Lepic mounted upwards to the rustic heights of Montmartre. It was astonishing how significant, coherent and understandable it all became after a glass of wine on an empty stomach.' Yes, Rhys is a choice novelist for that perennial category of reader: the vicarious drinker. If you were to play the *Withnail and I* game of having a drink every time the characters do, you'd be sloshed after ten pages. Her books' cover designs often boast variations on a simple theme: glass of booze on a wooden table.

Rhys herself had a considerable talent for unhappiness (and for drinking). *Quartet* initiates a journey into previously uncharted territories of female desperation, where the line blurs between exploiter and exploited, and there's never enough love to go around.

What I didn't know on first reading it is that Quartet *was a revenge novel, one of many that pepper literary history. Back before they had hashtags, Rhys wrote it to impugn the character of her mentor Ford Maddox Ford – he's the basis for H.J. Heidler, and everybody knew it – who she felt had exploited her, though he was of the view that it takes two to tango. Ford retaliated with his own novelised version of their affair, making Rhys out to be a vindictive and manipulative drunk. Beneath the he-said-she-said smoke and fire, there is a maxim to be extracted from all this: you should never sleep with writers, because if you do you will end up in their books. You may think you'll be pleased to end up in their books, but this only means you've forgotten that it's they and not you who decide how you'll appear. The caveat is that, if you too happen to be a writer, the matter won't end there: you will have the option of retaliating at will, delivering the next blow in an escalating series of aggressions that could end in suicide or murder. It will play out like a Twitter spat in slow motion, or a rap beef with diss tracks hurled back and forth, only to a much smaller audience. The deeper truth here is that the key consolation of being a writer is that* nothing bad can really happen to you. *Or rather, a great many terrible things can and undoubtedly will happen to you, but in your deepest core you will remain pristine, impregnable, because there is nothing you can experience that cannot be transmuted into living prose, the way the alchemists transmuted base metals into gold. The innumerable disasters that befall each writer will in the end* leave you shattered, welcoming the repose of death. But this whimpering wretch you've become, numb from kicks and scorn, will have bifurcated its deeper being and thus saved itself: on one hand, there is the cringing broken animal, and on the other, the evacuated spirit, immutable in words.

14 URSULA K. LE GUIN

The Dispossessed (1974)

Let's break science fiction into three broad and non-exclusive categories: there is the sort that deals with the truly Other; the 'hard' sort that cleaves to actual science; and the sort that utilises the genre's imaginative freedoms to comment on contemporary society. Ursula K. Le Guin's work tends to fall into the third category, though she bristled at the science fiction label, telling a *Paris Review* interviewer: 'My tentacles are coming out of the pigeonhole in all directions.' Towards the end of her life, Le Guin championed younger trailblazers like China Miéville, and campaigned against science fiction's assumed inferiority to the genre of 'literary fiction'.

Le Guin's novels explored her manifold intellectual passions, which included Taoism, feminism, anthropology and political philosophy. *The Dispossessed*'s helical structure bounces us back and forth between two very different planets: Urras, with its cruel 'propertarian' hierarchies, and Anarres, a parched moon run on anarchist principles. The set-up facilitates an enduringly profitable thought experiment: how would life under capitalism appear to someone who did not take its ideology and mode of living for granted?

Shevek is a physicist of Anarres, where renegades from Urras established independence more than a century ago. Stifled by the all-too-human pettiness of his Anarresian comrades, he travels to Urras to finish developing a means of instantaneous communication. Welcomed like a rock star and invited to live the Urrasian way, Shevek doesn't like what he sees: down here it's all hangovers and infidelity and contempt for the poor. It's tempting to describe *The Dispossessed* as a classic of leftist science fiction but, due to its integrity as a novel, it isn't that simple. I read it when I still suspected that my anarcho-punk friends might be right about everything. While *The Dispossessed* rammed home the ways in which capitalism mutilates us, life in the anarchist 'utopia' of Anarres – hard labour, dust and aggressively policed mediocrity – made me wonder if capitalism wasn't the best of a bad lot.

When I was a disturbed twenty-year-old I fell in with some punks who set up a squat in a vacant Georgian building in Dublin. I visited the place a few times; I remember a sign on a wall saying Don't Be an Idiot – Read a Book. *I formed a band with a friend who'd moved into the squat: a wiry Marxist intellectual and former heroin addict from the United States who'd come to Ireland with his girlfriend, a porn actress. Having no interest in playing straightforward punk or hardcore the way my bandmates would have done if left to their own inclinations, I tugged the band towards a weird and disorientating sound built on what I considered a pioneering style of guitar playing (it involved bright-toned power chords coupled with aggressive whammy-bar manipulation). At an early practice session we wondered what we should call ourselves. I suggested The Rolling Stones and it was settled. When I lived in London years later, one of my closest friends was another punk, Cormac, who knew the guys who'd set up the Dublin squat (I'd long since lost touch with them). Cormac lived in a squat in Brixton with his girlfriend, whereas I lived on the opposite, north-eastern side of the city. Occasionally I rode the underground beneath central London and across the Thames to enjoy parties thrown by the couple. These were wild, debauched, amphetamine-fuelled revels that kicked off on Friday and lasted three days, at which point Cormac and I would stagger into the language school in Bayswater where we both worked as English teachers, to shakily instruct our multi-ethnic students in grammar and pronunciation. I taught only one lesson per day, so that I would have*

61

time and energy to write. This meant I lived in squalor and had no money. One afternoon in a pub in Portobello, Cormac told me a story about things he'd seen and done in Mexico, a tale notable for its high quotient of violence and moral decay. A few weeks later, I wrote down what I half remembered of it as a short story, which I went on to publish. He never seemed to hold it against me. These days he lives in Australia, where he and his now wife have two little girls who I see sometimes on Instagram. His hardcore band tours Europe, Japan, the USA. I travelled from Berlin by train to see them play at a squat in Bremen. Their set was over in half an hour: a furious cathartic blast, a squeal of feedback and the applause of faded punks who have found some happiness in life.

15 NORMAN MAILER

The Fight (1975)

In a recent *Irish Times* article Norman Mailer was written off as 'a bad joke'. Mailer, with his *oeuvre* as big, brash and brilliant as the American century that birthed him! The goad cannot pass unchallenged, so here I am in Norman's corner, pouring water in his mouth and rubbing his shoulders till he gets back up for another round.

There are two kinds of reader I can imagine loving *The Fight* as much as I do: those who have an interest in boxing, and everybody else. Mailer's account of the 1974 heavyweight championship fight in Zaire between Muhammad Ali and George Foreman has all the dramatic tension of a novel even though we know how it's going to end. Mailer is no disembodied observer: 'Now, our man of wisdom had a vice. He wrote about himself. Not only would he describe the events he saw, but his own small effect on events.'

Mailer has been sunk in unfashion since a literary generation of American Nice Guys derided him and his peers as the Great American Narcissists. With writing this incandescent, though, one can wait confidently for the decrees of public taste to veer back around. From the opening paragraph, Mailer's pugilistic prose comes out swinging to mark the human glory of Mohammad Ali: 'Women draw an *audible* breath. Men look *down*. They are reminded again of their lack of worth.'

The stink of testosterone is high, with nary a female in sight as Mailer stakes out both camps in the weeks before the fight, drinking and bantering with Don King, Hunter Thompson, Joe Frazier. Mailer realises he is not there merely to cover a fight. With a reckless candour foreign to today's eggshell-walking writers, he probes 'his own outsized feelings of love and – could it be? – sheer hate for the existence of Black on earth.' The fight itself reads as a planet-quaking clash between two black gods. Little wonder Mailer has such sympathy for these titans: he fell on his ass a few times, but he only ever wrote like a heavyweight.

In terms of structure as well as attitude, the book by Norman Mailer I find most stimulating is not The Fight *but* Advertisements for Myself. *It's as audacious as Kanye West at his maniacal peak, a book of startling presumption and egoism that consists of the essays, interventions, slanders, bellicose magazine columns and other writings that Mailer had produced by the age of thirty-six, when he decided to clear the decks before embarking on another novel. Crucially, these writings are not simply presented on their own terms, as would be the case with a more modest writer's miscellany. Each piece is prefaced by an italicised passage in which Mailer ruthlessly analyses the internal and external factors that had been working on him when he wrote it. Together these amount to a patchwork memoir of literary success, crisis and evolution that Mailer subtitles 'Biography of a Style'. It's a daring public self-analysis, with Mailer as unsparing of himself as he is of his rivals and adversaries (even more than half a century later, the pitiless but astute hot takes in 'Evaluations – Quick and Expensive Comments on the Talent in the Room' can still raise the temperature). While plenty of the inclusions beg to be skipped – in his scoldy introduction Mailer actually invites us to skip them – the italicised interstitial sections are gripping. Those are the real story of the book, its spine and central nervous system, rather than, say, the short stories Mailer wrote while at college and which he chucks in as a courtesy to PhD candidates. Nestled within the disjointed memoir is a lengthy account of the writing and publication of Mailer's third novel,* The Deer Park.

I haven't got the slightest interest in reading the novel itself, but Mailer's candour in narrativising its creation is compulsive. He betrays a near obsessive – or just egomaniacal – interest in his own thought processes, and has no doubt that his readers will find them just as fascinating. This account of the writing of a book that makes the reading of the book itself superfluous, compels me to imagine a writer – a monster-mutation of the Mailer strain – who produces just a slim novel or two, then spends the rest of a prolific career dramatising their gestation in a sort of oeuvre-sized origin myth. And then I realise that this writer already exists – it's that bearded and ubiquitous Viking, Karl Ove Knausgaard. The craggy Norwegian notwithstanding, no male writer will again write with Mailer's imperial self-importance, not for a hundred years at least – which, after a long session on the receiving end of Mailer's smack-talking bluster, is cause for relief. Male writers now are the opposition party, and that may not be such a bad thing for them. New visions and strange perspectives will emerge from the ghettos of a chastened masculinity.

16 J.K. HUYSMANS

À rebours (1884)

Translated by Robert Baldick

This novel is evil. I read it in Bolivia, and that same evening I ate a portion of San Pedro, the hallucinatory cactus that grows on the altiplano. I spent the night cowering in the corner of the room, as J.K. Huysmans's cadaverous vision suffocated me with tentacles of unspeakable hideousness. To say it got under my skin will not suffice: it got into my soul, and never quite left. With his portrait of Des Esseintes – an impotent aristocrat so disgusted by modern life and human stupidity that he retreats into solipsistic, rarefied sensualism in a chateau on the edge of Paris – Huysmans drags the reader into an airless and morbid universe. The exhaustion and spleen that choke these pages feel not local but ontological. You can't go in there and remain unscathed.

Huysmans's middle finger to humanity marked his break with the naturalist movement, and the apex of French decadence. *À rebours* was a scandal not only for its disturbing content, but for its plotless defiance of novelistic convention. At the outset, Des Esseintes is 'utterly alone, completely disillusioned, abominably tired; and he longed to make an end to it all'. He doesn't like other people: 'The human face as glimpsed in the street had been one of the keenest torments he had been forced to endure.' Logically enough, he is the novel's only character.

In the pitch of its misanthropy and its aura of utter damnation, *À rebours* strikes me as a kind of nineteenth-century

American Psycho – the type of book that hangs over the culture like a bad smell. Its chapters detail the ever-more refined means by which Des Esseintes stimulates his jaded nervous system. There are flowers; there is perfume; there is classical literature and symbolist poetry; there is a tortoise whose shell is encrusted with diamonds.

Absurd? More than a little. And yet, sequestered in our private digital cocoons, relieved at no longer having to face our neighbours, we've all gone a bit Des Esseintes lately. 'Nature, he used to say, has had her day.'

On the Bolivian altiplano is a town called Tupiza, which in the zone where desire and memory converge stands on the threshold of South American dreamtime. It's a silent, melancholy, dusty town, a couple of hundred people surrounded by desert and red-rock canyons. When I was twenty-four I passed through Tupiza after a period spent ill and immobile in Argentina. Only, I didn't really pass through, I slowed right down, ground to a halt, found myself standing at a node of absolute stillness. Tupiza was my gateway to the revelation that Bolivia exists apart from the rest of South America – a sorrowful and unearthly country, landlocked and elevated, a dream within a mythic-geological dream. When you cross its border you phase into a different schema of perception, enter a place you seem to recognise from submerged childhood memories or some deep portal in the collective knowing. I hung around Tupiza for a few weeks, convalescing. In the evenings I drank red wine from cartons, getting spectacularly drunk due to the altitude and my weakened condition. By day I walked to the edge of the town and out into the red-rock landscape. There I would lie on the earth, look up into the vastness of blue, doze off. An eagle soars past, a cactus looms. A whisper of wind. The sun warm on my skin. Later I would write a novel, which I never bothered showing anyone, about a young man drifting across South America. There was no story, no drama. Writing the novel was really a pretext to try and get back there, to Tupiza; that deep-time stillness, that solitary exaltation surrounded by obliterating blue and powdery red. I ought not to have had my narrator wander any further, board a bus or train, but stay right there, where he is on the first page: the dusty earth on the edge of a town on the high plains, gazing up at a vertical sun in a pristine sky, exactly where he longs to be.

17 ANNIE DILLARD

Holy the Firm (1977)

Many writers display an acute interest in human beings, but remarkably little interest in whatever it is that lies *behind* human beings and the world in which they manifest – that is, in metaphysics. Not so Annie Dillard. She tends to be described as a nature writer, though for her it is not nature but Creation. At her darkest, she comes near to echoing Charlotte Gainsbourg's character in Lars von Trier's panic attack of a film *Antichrist*, who declares that 'nature is the church of Satan'.

Holy the Firm may not be Dillard's most successful book, but it is surely her oddest: a characteristically intemperate, indeed hysterical, act of communion with the Pacific coastal landscape of Puget Sound in Washington State, where Dillard lived alone for two years in a room as 'plain as a skull'. Dillard's religiousness is no meek adherence to the flock, but an appalled, ecstatic opening of the self to God's radiant terror as expressed in the savage immensity of the natural world. She writes in the panoramic, unembarrassable American high style of Emerson and Kerouac. Some readers will have had enough after the first sentence: 'Every day is a god, each day is a god, and holiness holds forth in time.'

'Nothing is going to happen in this book,' she insists early on, with only 'a little violence here and there in the language'. This is not quite true. Dillard endeavours to describe everything that occurs in her elemental retreat over three days.

On the second day, a plane crashes, 'and Julie Norwich seven years old burnt off her face.' The tragedy sparks not so much a crisis of faith, as a furious attack on God as a divine terrorist, or a weakling, or a 'kenotic suicide'. *Holy the Firm* is a prayer from the overwhelmed, with Dillard professing the romantic credo of the writer as one who is all-in, self-contemptuous as a martyr. Finally, 'There is no such thing as an artist: there is only the world, lit or unlit as the light allows.'

We are in the teeth of the outbreak now, the virus spreading fast across the planet and here I am, stranded and solitary in a half-deserted port town, no possible company for weeks ahead, time stretching before me like the cliffs and coastline past the harbour. I live online, I listen to news of cities around the globe where the contagion is peaking, the dead carried out in military trucks for mass cremation. Today the clocks went forward. Each afternoon, after writing a page or two, I fold the screen and leave my phone at home and walk out on the beach. The ferries still sail in and out of the harbour, bound for Santander and Normandy and Wales. The surf foams over golden sand, and where my senses merge with memory this Wexford coast becomes overlaid with other beaches from past lives: Ocean Beach in San Francisco, where the Pacific is too cold to swim; a beach on a Thai island where the gulf waters were postcard blue; beaches in Dublin in the summers of childhood; the one in Peru where I slept after arriving in town late, and in the dawn a figure approached from the distance, silhouetted against the rooftops. My days haven't changed much since the pandemic transformed life on earth in a matter of weeks, in an unfolding that is at the same time global and intimately local. I do what I've always done, the difference being that now I don't have a choice, can't create all those diversions for myself. There are no appointments on my calendar. I haven't booked any train to Dublin from a habitual urge to hang out with friends or wander in the city. What seemed essential is revealed to only ever have been optional, superfluous. The days are entirely mine to fill, to wander in like I wander on the beach where I idled in yesterday's evening sun, watching the surf. It makes me feel I could live this way indefinitely and I'd be all right; that I've done enough living and can now spend my time holding up the memories for contemplation, determining what it all meant. Images flood in: cities I've passed through; rooms where I've slept; friends who put me up or put up with me. In a couple of years I'll turn forty. Schopenhauer wrote that the first forty years are the text, the rest is the commentary. I see that, and yet I feel that I'm somehow at the start of a life, on the cusp, facing a future that's strange and turbulent but not entirely hopeless.

18 SUSAN SONTAG

Against Interpretation and Other Essays (1966)

When I watched the 2014 documentary *Regarding Susan Sontag*, the ending struck me as a disturbing parable of the Western intellectual condition. Sontag, a woman as erudite as anybody in the twentieth century, is informed that she is dying of cancer. She refuses to believe it, hoping for a miracle cure. After further tests, her doctor confirms that death is imminent. Faced with this certitude that permits no denial, Sontag screams. The knowledge amassed over a lifetime spent 'in the search for aesthetic bliss' has no worth now: it has not transmuted into wisdom. She panics until the end.

But then, isn't it the consolation of the writer or the artist that death, though terrifying, can't really hurt you? If you've worked hard enough, you'll have delivered everything precious into safekeeping – the ransacking won't touch it. In the 1960s, Sontag moved to New York after a period spent living in France, and there 'began to discharge some of the cargo of ideas' generated over thirty years of cultural voracity into a collection of essays. Her evangelical Europhilia helped dent what Milan Kundera called 'the provincialism of large nations', which was rampant in a United States puffed up on economic growth and imperial expansion.

The drift of the superb title essay will find favour among artists. We betray works of art, Sontag argues, when we compulsively seek to answer that dreary question, *What does it mean?* The value of a work lies not in some allegorical shadow-story into which it must be deciphered, but in the emotional and sensuous response it elicits in its audience.

Many of the figures who Sontag championed in the sixties have since become canonical. Her critical intelligence is vivified by often striking metaphor, as in this opening to an essay on Albert Camus: 'Great writers are either husbands or lovers. Some writers supply the solid virtues of a husband: reliability, intelligibility, generosity, decency... Notoriously, women tolerate qualities in a lover – moodiness, selfishness, unreliability, brutality – that they would never countenance in a husband, in return for excitement, an infusion of intense feeling.'

8A STOCK ORCHARD CRESCENT, LONDON N7: On my first night living in London, a few weeks before my twenty-seventh birthday, I slept in a garden while a light rain fell, lying on my backpack to keep off the concrete pathway. Through the basement window I could see the bed that was mine to take, if only I could find the key my friend had left out for me, somewhere in the garden. It must have come to me in a dream: at dawn, I rose creakily to my feet and, without hesitation, retrieved the key from beneath a certain tile. Through the back door I let myself into the appallingly filthy house I was to sublet from my friend. Only a little dog named Henry was there to greet me. Later that day, I cleared the desk in my bedroom and wrote the first lines of what I hoped would be a novel. Several weeks later, my then girlfriend came to visit from America. During her stay, she wrote a poem entitled '8A Stock Orchard Crescent'. In the poem, she and I fought acidly, and stormed off in contrary directions along a dark street on an October evening.

39 EADE ROAD, LONDON N4 1DJ: When the friend from whom I was subletting returned, I moved into the cheapest place I could find. This was a mistake. In London, even horrid flats rent for absurd amounts: if a place is being let for a pittance, there's a reason for it. The house was on a quiet street near Finsbury Park. My room was one of the few I've ever seen that merited the epithet 'box room'. Among my eight housemates were the aforementioned Vulgarians – two couples. Around dinnertime the kitchen would become crowded, a bottle of rakia would appear and the genocidal folk songs would begin in earnest. These were interpreted for me by a backslapping patriot confident I would endorse his tribal enthusiasms. I remember one song in particular – a boisterous ditty about a tank commander who drove over a camp full of gypsies. Soon the living situation soured. There were threats and stand-offs; a bread knife was brandished. It took more time and energy to cycle to the language school on the other side of the city than it did to teach my one class there. When I got home around noon, I would eat ravenously, then doze on the couch with earplugs in to muffle the Slav-trance booming from the bedroom of my DJ housemate. Refreshed, I would fix a flask of coffee and cycle to the library to spend the rest of the day writing. My girlfriend came to stay in the summer. Almost a year had passed since we'd been together. I decided that this was no house in which to host a female.

FLAT 97, WOOLRIDGE WAY TOWER BLOCKS, LODDIGES ROAD, LONDON E8: Another couple I knew were leaving town for a while, so they let us house-sit their council flat in a high-rise off Mare Street. They were subletting from a man who I only ever heard referred to as Peter Pan. He was long-term unemployed, terminally ill and had lately gone to Thailand for an indeterminate period. Strictly speaking, it was illegal for Peter Pan to sublet his council flat, but there was no other way he could have gone off to Asia without losing it. I never met Peter Pan, but I did see a photo of him on an ID card: late fifties, with lank, silvery hair. Periodically he emailed my friend about the drugs he was taking and the girls he was having sex with. He had gone to Thailand in the awareness of his impending death, with the frank intention of enjoying a prolonged debauch. We stayed at that flat for a few balmy weeks, raising an aperitif at dusk to Peter Pan and his comforters. The rear balcony looked onto a courtyard that was closed in on four sides by tower blocks, where children played throughout the day. Perched halfway up each block was a motion-sensing camera that whirred about constantly, as if pepped up on Ritalin. My girlfriend flew to Boston to begin an MFA in poetry – we planned to reunite in the winter – and I moved into a house in Hackney.

58 NARFORD ROAD, LONDON E5 8RD: I've just used Google Maps to street-view the house where I lived for a couple of years, just down from Stoke Newington High Street and the basement nightclubs of Dalston. The window of the living room is still boarded up – we never got around to sorting that out – while bins and buckets clutter the strip of cement that passed for our front garden. I will have more to say on my time at this address later, so for now I'll fast-forward to when I moved out and followed my girlfriend to San Francisco (fresh out of college in Boston, she'd taken a job there at American Apparel).

109 SOUTH END CLOSE, LONDON NW3 2RE: We moved back to London the following winter, after six troubled months in California. Once again we were subletting less than legally – this time from an American in his sixties who had written a book on Jack the Ripper, and his girlfriend, a graphic novelist. The cave-like flat on the fifth floor of a block next to Hampstead

Heath was crammed with books (the couple also ran a stall on Hampstead High Street). The views over the London skyline were entrancing, especially at night. I got into the habit of lurking by the window with the lights off, a pair of binoculars pressed to my face, peering in the windows of distant blocks or at the lit-up skyscrapers of the City and Canary Wharf. My girlfriend's highly traditional Vietnamese parents had been against her moving back to England with me, and against our planned marriage, and against my very existence, or so I'd come to imagine. We never did get married. Near the end of her six-month visa, I came home one day to find her gone, together with her belongings. She returned to the USA and I never saw her again.

20B FINSBURY PARK ROAD, LONDON N4 2JZ: For my last ten days in London, I stayed with the friend in whose garden I'd slept four years earlier. He had moved a few blocks away, to a street near the park. On my last night we stayed up drinking whiskey and listening to the album we had recorded together, recently finished. I slept for an hour or two, woke hung-over, and was lucky not to miss the train that took me away from the city, across the British countryside, to the ferry port at Holyhead. It is difficult, when we look back on certain periods of our lives, not to succumb to romanticism and nostalgia. Even while I lived in London, though, I romanticised the city and the life I lived there; or rather, I knew it was a beautiful, romantic time of life, and that, like youth itself, the circumstances that had come so magically together would never be repeated, and that one day I would regret those years. Although I sometimes tantalise myself with the idea of *moving to London again, I don't need Heraclitus to remind me that you can't step into the same city twice. The London where I lived no longer exists, any more than a dream exists upon awakening – a dream in which you were happy, in which life lived up to its promise.*

19 GEORGES BATAILLE

Erotism: Death and Sensuality (1957)

Translated by Mary Dalwood

Even by the standards of French literature, Georges Bataille was a serious pervert. He was also, at least for part of his life, mad. Pornographic novels such as *The Story of the Eye* and *Blue of Noon*, and bizarre early texts such as 'The Solar Anus', betray not only the influence of surrealism, a movement with which Bataille was fractiously involved, but evidence of a genuinely sick mind. If Bataille did not become an influential twentieth-century thinker, we might instead be reading about him in true-crime books detailing abominable acts.

While some of Bataille's writings are scarcely coherent – I say that as an admirer – his late theoretical work *Erotism* is a surprisingly cogent, wide-ranging examination of the obsessions Bataille pursued his whole life long. A devout Christian who abandoned the faith and hurled himself into a mysticism of evil, Bataille sought an atheistic basis for ecstatic experience that would redeem humankind from enslavement to work, security and acquisition. To him, we are anguished, 'discontinuous' beings who seek fusion with the universe by way of eroticism, which in its fullest expression approaches death. *Erotism* pulls in materials from a variety of disciplines – art history, sociology, anthropology – to back up Bataille's vision of a cosmos consumed by raging violence, where loss and devastation must be embraced.

Having abandoned his blind, incontinent father to the approaching German forces during the First World War, Bataille sought forbidden knowledge in the foulest of extremities. Human sacrifice, organised war and festivals of cruelty would have their place in any society unwise enough to let him call the shots. During the Second World War, he did in fact establish a notorious secret society, Acéphale, whose members met in a forest outside Paris, where they may or may not have conducted disturbing rites (their highest aspiration was to perform a human sacrifice).

Proceed with caution: *Erotism* is a fascinating abyss that gazes back, a book you might wish to seal and bury deep underground, where it would contaminate the earth with putrefactive visions of excess.

A curious reversal can befall us as we pass through life, whereby the authors we once turned to in order to be shocked out of sedation and consensus – in my case, Nietzsche, Schopenhauer, Bataille, Houellebecq – become, by virtue of the world's mutation into threatening and unfamiliar forms, sources of nostalgia, comfort reading. Another way to say it is that the male, isolationist authors I wagered on in my youth have left me painfully ill-equipped for life in the glare of the feminist, hive-minded 2020s. Perhaps it's an inevitable ache of ageing, the karmic slap-down whereby we who once assailed sacred truth ourselves become the assailed, and the authors who egged us on come to seem a liability – or as E.M. Cioran put it, in youth we are furious to overthrow everything, but soon we find we're next to be overthrown. Like the American I recently read about who sued his parents for giving him life (a reader of Cioran?), I might one day file a lawsuit against the great writers who led me astray in my twenties – those contrarians and arch provocateurs. I feel taken advantage of. They were all talk, they left me seduced and abandoned. Maybe the shrieking pink-haired campus ideologues I habitually ridicule have a point, and my grave and caustic Europeans really are just dead white men, vampire-sentries to a dead white civilisation – and now we need new masters.

20 NATHALIE SARRAUTE

Tropisms (1939)

Translated by Maria Jolas

When all I knew of the *nouveau roman* was the work of Alain
Robbe-Grillet, I felt about it as I do about erotic practices
involving ropes and clamps: I didn't doubt that others got
their kicks from it, but it wasn't really for me. As performed
by Robbe-Grillet, the radical attempt to turn away from the
nineteenth-century novel of plots and characters involved
cold, meticulous descriptions of external objects, which is
exactly as riveting as it sounds.

Nathalie Sarraute's *Tropisms*, however, is alluringly strange.
Sarraute's first book and the *nouveau roman*'s foundational
text, *Tropisms* is a slim novel that took five years to write.
It depicts in twenty-four vignettes the doings of assorted,
unnamed figures in an oneiric landscape that is by turns
oppressive and mundane, 'an existence like a waiting room
in a deserted suburban railway station'. Sarraute wrote each
piece in order to express in image and drama the pre-verbal,
'instinctual movements' that, she thought, arise from the
unconscious and 'constitute the secret source of our existence'. A fellow denizen of Left Bank cafés, Jean-Paul Sartre
reportedly said of Sarraute's work, 'it is existence itself'.

Taking the modernist interiorities of Proust, Woolf and
Joyce to a deeper, weirder place, *Tropisms* is a literary echo of
painting's move towards abstraction. Despite Sarraute's insistence on the work's hermetic, essential nature, a recognisable

world glancingly shines through the slats. Here and there, proper nouns appear amid the mysterious toings and froings: locations in Paris, famous writers.

The term 'tropisms', which in biology denotes the motions of plants and organisms prompted by external stimuli, became a lifelong meme for Sarraute. Her ambition to observe and express these unconscious movements never abated. If Sarraute did not explain her intentions in the theoretical essays she began writing in the late 1940s, would we understand *Tropisms* to be the imagistic expression of inner 'tropisms'? And if not, does that diminish the work's value? More uncertainties, provoked by a novel that imprints the mind with the shape of a question mark.

Now why on earth did I choose this slight novel by Nathalie Sarraute when there were so many more personally significant, less anorexic books I could have chosen? The answer is simple: I chose it because it is very short. I am a slow reader and, pressed for time, I didn't have it in me that week to reread War and Peace *and write about that. When you are as slow a reader as I am, you have to choose your battles, and rereading* War and Peace *was a battle I lost before it began. Besides, I like short books. The shorter the better, really. Most books outstay their welcome, still talking at you while you stifle a yawn. I admire writers who at least try to live up to Nietzsche's cunning boast that he could say in ten sentences what other writers say in whole books – what other writers* do not say *in whole books. It used to do my head in that I was such a slow reader. I used to think how wonderful it would be if I could tear through hundreds of books per year; how much more knowledgeable I'd become. Like many of the hang-ups and manias of youth, that has fallen away. There's no rush. We're not going anywhere. In the old world, the world before the virus, we were all racing off somewhere, eager to be in another city or country where life might seem more meaningful, but it turns out there's nowhere we need to be, here is fine. So I may as well take my time, savour, linger, luxuriate. Besides, reading books, I sometimes feel, is only the foreplay to the deeper pleasure of rereading them. As some other writer has no doubt already said – Susan Sontag, probably – if a book is worth reading only once it's hardly worth reading at all.*

21 E.M. CIORAN

The Trouble with Being Born (1973)

Translated by Richard Howard

E.M. Cioran is the most addictive writer I've ever encountered. At the height of my fixation, anything I read that *wasn't* him felt anodyne, trivial and long-winded. Born in Romania, Cioran wrote most of his savagely pessimistic books in French, having moved to Paris in the 1930s and settled into a 'parasitical' life there. His writing desecrates humanity, progress, virtue, reality itself, and anything else that looked at him funny. Cioran lays it on so thick, the rancour is so extravagant, you start to wonder if he's taking the piss. And that's the thing: the writing is relentless and splenetic and nihilistic, but it's never devoid of humour – a stand-up routine at the gates of hell.

As a stylist, Cioran has as much flair as anyone who has written, and nowhere more so than in the aphorisms that make up *The Trouble with Being Born*, an orgy of cynicism and philosophical violence that circles around a ludicrous jibe: Cioran's insistence that the thing to be avoided at all costs is – yes! – getting born. The renewal of species is an endless holocaust, and in this 'fallen universe' the one unpardonable crime is to inflict life on the unborn.

No summary of Cioran's thought can do justice to the visceral euphoria of reading him. Most of his ideas repackage the Eastern metaphysics of the Void and the Western sceptical traditions in which he was steeped; the distinction lies in his mode of attack, his ecstatic spleen. Scattered with autobiographical glimpses of a man at a comical extremity of torment, *Trouble* riffs on Cioran's favourite themes: suicide; metaphysical exile; disdain for humankind ('that hideous and immemorial riffraff'); civilisational decline; the unreality of existence; and the wisdom of cultivating 'the long serene disgust of detachment'.

For all his scepticism, Cioran strikes me as an essentially religious thinker, transfixed by ultimate questions, although for him any divine architect is a drunkard and a hooligan, at fault for a 'botched Creation' wherein even suicide isn't worth the effort, because it always comes *too late*.

In a portentously soundtracked documentary about his life and work that can be viewed on YouTube, an aged but still impishly handsome Cioran is asked why he has stopped writing books. It's very simple, he replies: he just got tired. Specifically, he says he got tired of 'slandering the universe' (he hadn't lost his turn of phrase), but of course what he really meant is that he got tired of waking each morning to ask himself whether he had anything to say and some fresh means of saying it. With on-brand curmudgeonliness he tells his interlocutor, 'All the writers wrote too much, in my opinion.' He himself would buck the trend. Personally, I'm not quite sure that Cioran's decade-long silence was entirely the real deal. By the time he made the decision not to write any more, he had already published lots of books, thus breathing life into a golem of reputation that he could fairly well trust to live on under its own momentum – and even to gain greater presence by his ostentatious refusal to add to the oeuvre. *When a writer has already achieved a lot, literary 'silence' entails neither an elected nor an unwilled obscurity, but may be a canny instalment in the ongoing production. Cioran's final decade amounted to a* performed *refusal; moreover, one that was philosophically in dialogue with his prior work, which made so much of the tendency to inertia and quietude. Cioran's was a silence assured of an audience, as the fact of a documentary filmmaker travelling from Romania to Paris to question him about it attests. Which is not to say that the elderly, refusenik Cioran didn't struggle with a more mundane problem facing any writer who chooses* not to write (or who is unable to): what to do with himself all day. Perhaps he was in a better position here than most, having already made his stance on the matter clear when he wrote, 'By all evidence we are in the world to do nothing.' In my own case, even though the act of putting words on a page in a seductive order requires effort, writing and doing nothing are by no means opposites – rather, they are two sides of the same coin, dimensions of one another. I've never shaken off the working-class notion that writing books is a way of making a living by shirking work, even if I habitually wear myself out by doing it, even if a nine-to-five job sometimes seems a less exhausting way to go about being in the world. But let's give the last word on all this to another aphorist, Lev Shestov, who suggested an answer to the question of why so many writers keep at it long after they've expressed whatever set them down at their desks in the first place:

> When a person is young he writes because it seems to him he has discovered a new almighty truth which he must make haste to impart to forlorn humankind. Later, becoming more modest, he begins to doubt his truths: and then he tries to convince himself. A few more years go by, and he knows he was mistaken all round, so there is no need to convince himself. Nevertheless he continues to write, because he is not fit for any other work, and to be accounted a superfluous person is so horrible.

94

22 ANGELA CARTER

The Bloody Chamber (1979)

The Bloody Chamber is a kind of applied literary psycho-analysis, in which Angela Carter retells ten fairy tales to uncover their 'violently sexual' latent content. Not that her blood-soaked renditions are a dry theoretical exercise: they are lusciously sensual, and the best of them are as enchanting as the childhood narratives on which they draw.

Carter was a contrary, elusive type of feminist who drew ire from her more puritanical peers, not least for her long essay *The Sadean Woman* (published the same year as *The Bloody Chamber*), in which she makes a spirited if ludicrous bid to reposition the Marquis de Sade as a proto-feminist figure (she approves of his enthusiasm for anal sex, which affirmed women as sexual beings independent of their reproductive function).

Sexuality as an incendiary force, and the intoxications of pain and annihilation recur throughout *The Bloody Chamber* like the ruminations of an obsessive. These tales of were-wolves, talking cats, sinister noblemen and necro-paedophiles recall in their gothic lyricism the songs of Nick Cave and the Bad Seeds; like Cave's lyrics, they portray desire as a satanic choreography in which we move irresistibly towards the site of our destruction. A narrator intones: 'Now you are at the place of annihilation, now you are at the place of annihilation.'

In Carter's realm, 'sheer carnal avarice' is the lifeblood, and innocence craves its own defilement. While subverting male power, Carter collaterally eviscerates that corruption of feminism whereby female desire is limpid, irreproachable, without darkness. A virginal girl says of a strange being who lives alone in the woods, 'I knew from the first moment I saw him how Erl-King would do me grievous harm', then goes to him anyway. In the wonderful titular story, another girl admits, 'in my heart I had always known' that the rich psychopath she has married 'would be the death of me'.

In short, these sadomasochistic stories roam the dark, offline places of the psyche – a black forest, too true to be good, where love is torture and lust is a bloodbath.

'Love is Torture': that is a good title and you might one day see it emblazoning the cover of a book with my name on it. Titles are interesting: their arbitrariness that becomes essential; the question of at what point during a work's elaboration the author decides on one, and how this in turn influences the work. Some titles precede *works and any notion of what they might contain. There are titles that exist for years in such a disembodied state, like the spirits that drift through the bardo awaiting incarnation. When I lived in France, a title occurred to me out of the blue, free of context and unattached to any particular work in progress. I didn't think much about what it meant, I only knew it was a good title. A year or two later, I gave the title to a short co-written book for which it was the perfect fit. Perhaps the title had even helped conceive and shape the work, in the mists below the threshold of awareness. Perhaps potential works are in this way like fruits ripe for plucking, as they await the titles that will draw them into the world. Conversely, it seems to me that culture is haunted by phantom titles, the great titles that were dreamed up and then abandoned, orphaned, so that they are condemned to wander the earth like unquiet souls. Kurt Cobain wanted to call what would become the final Nirvana album not* In Utero *but* I Hate Myself and Want to Die. *Krist Novoselic and Dave Grohl, more prudent and perhaps less pure, managed to talk him down. What a pity. How violent a statement of distress and self-contempt Cobain's title would have been, both primed for the grungy moment and timelessly abject. Likewise, Kanye West intended the follow-up record to*

Yeezus *to be titled* So Help Me God, *but changed his mind and called it* The Life of Pablo. *As with the Nirvana album, I can't think about Kanye's discarded title without a pang of regret – its dualism of desperation and reverence, defiance and supplication. I can imagine a book that consists* only *of titles and subtitles, in the way that Édouard Levé composed an entire book of concepts for non-existent artworks.*

23 ALEXANDER TROCCHI

Cain's Book (1960)

The fact that after publishing his scarcely fictionalised account of junkie-existentialist detachment, *Cain's Book*, at age thirty-five, having spent his apprentice years cultivating powerful literary friends and dazzling everyone with his sense of embodied promise, Alexander Trocchi never wrote another book, suggests that what he was doing all along was preparing the ground not for his future work's reception, but for the fact of its falling short – in other words, that Trocchi's deeply willed destiny was to fail with an audience. In this sense, we might read *Cain's Book* as a secondary text, a commentary on the silence that followed across decades of private disintegration.

There is no story to tell, no message of hope or improvement. A man from Europe spends his days shooting heroin on a scow docked at a harbour in New York, occasionally bestirring himself to add a few pages to *Cain's Book*, 'the product of those moments when I felt impelled to outflank my deep desire to be silent, to say nothing, expose nothing'. The pages drift past, monotonous and stark and radiant, a stalled narrative that bobs on the ripples while the narrator gazes indifferently at the Manhattan skyline. Heroin has made him sovereign, impregnable. 'For the attitude born of this sense of inviolability, some Americans have used the word "cool".'

Like heroin, writing is enlisted not to diminish the formlessness of existence, but to sink deeper into it, dissolving all sense of life's narrative quality. As still and flat as the

Hudson River lies 'the endless tundra which is all there is to be explored'. Incidents and memories sometimes disturb the impassive surface: a bleak night in London; scenes from childhood; years in Parisian bohemia; the seduction of a one-legged woman. All of them pass; the void reasserts itself.

This kind of book, with its air of existentialist machismo and self-regard, is wide open to ridicule – and electrifying on the same account. Trocchi took life and himself seriously enough to wreck both, with literature understood as subordinate, an accomplice to that wrecking.

In Irish society, heroin is a reliable class signifier, consumed only by the downtrodden, the lumpenproletariat. It's possible there are cultivated, bourgeois junkies too, but if so there aren't many of them, and they keep a low profile. The same class segregation applies to crack cocaine, which hasn't penetrated bohemian circles the way it has in, say, London. One exception is a friend of mine who sometimes smokes crack while doing yoga. This man is ten years my elder, a tech boffin and an autodidact, a devotee of science fiction and old 2000 AD comics. Sometimes we stroll in Phoenix Park and he talks at me with maniacal zeal, a torrent of conspiracy theories about the shadowy or incompetent forces ravaging our society. He is not on the side of the angels: beneath the bluster, his true political affiliation is with chaos. He works for a tech company, one of the Big Five, and his employers may or may not know that he is a viewer of reactionary YouTubers, a reader of politically questionable subreddits, a voter for the greater of two evils, a crack smoker. When we walk in the deer-inhabited park at dusk he gesticulates wildly with both hands, spilling coffee (he once told me he needs a double espresso to sleep). I've known him since I was a teenager, when he lived in a dilapidated house in the middle of an industrial estate. It was crammed with cables and recording equipment, and my friend threw raucous parties fuelled by weed and mescaline. I played in bands that recorded at the house, my friend acting as sound engineer. Sometimes we made short films there. Eventually it all burned to the ground when my friend's schizophrenic housemate left the toaster on while taking a nap.

24 MARCUS AURELIUS

Meditations (*c.* AD 160–181)

Translated by Martin Hammond

Some books compel our interest on account not only of their content, but of the remarkable nature of their production. Marcus Aurelius's *Meditations* comprises a niche literary genre unto itself: the philosophical self-help book written by a Roman emperor. The twelve books of *Meditations* are Marcus Aurelius's notes to self: it appears he never intended them for publication, but rather as auto-exhortations to 'be a man worthy of the universe that gave you birth'. *Meditations* is both a portrait of a noble spirit struggling with its all-too-human frailties, and an ageless road map for those seeking to live a virtuous life.

Marcus Aurelius lived and ruled in the second century AD, when the ideals of Stoicism held sway over the Roman court. He takes stock of himself – 'a male, mature in years, a statesman, a Roman, a ruler' – and goads himself to a sense of urgency: 'There is a limit circumscribed to your time – if you do not use it to clear away your clouds, it will be gone, and you will be gone, and the opportunity will not return.' As a Stoic, clearing away the clouds meant submitting to the laws of nature, accepting transience and death, and cultivating kindness towards friends and enemies alike. There is no sense seeking refuge from the world's strife 'in the country, by the sea, in the hills… when it is open to you, at any time you want, to retreat into yourself'.

Judging by the frequency with which he denounces it, it seems that the worldly adornment most tempting to Marcus Aurelius was fame. 'What then, will a little fame distract you? Look at the speed of universal oblivion, the gulf of immeasurable time both before and after, the vacuity of applause, the indiscriminate fickleness of your apparent supporters, the tiny room in which all this is confined.' He insists that rather than pursue vacuous applause, the wise should devote their efforts to becoming good. After all, 'Soon you will have forgotten all things: soon all things will have forgotten you.'

On the same trip during which Alice and I visited the piazza in Turin where Nietzsche collapsed into madness, we stayed for a while in Rome (Alice being my French translator, though she is a novelist too and a more successful one than me, so calling her my French translator is a little demeaning, a touch of post-break-up shade-throwing). My abiding memory of that sojourn is how much of it I've forgotten, save for a few generic grand-tour images – the Colosseum, the Trevi Fountain, the Forum – ruins monumentally propped against a brilliant August sky. One thing I do remember from Rome is that it was very hot, very hot indeed. Scorching, sweltering – all those adjectives apply. August is when it reliably gets so hot that the Romans clear out, and I spent most of our stay complaining to Alice about how hot it was, as if she were to blame. Another thing I remember is what I read while I was in Rome – more accurately, what I did not read, namely Marcus Aurelius, among countless other authors. It's possible, indeed highly likely, that I didn't read anything while I was in Rome, as even thinking about reading would have made me break into a torpid sweat. In general, I'm a faithful practitioner of site-specific reading, using books to enhance my experience of being in a place. Maybe it wasn't just the heat that put me off reading Marcus Aurelius in Rome. Perhaps I was still rattled by a prior instance of site-specific reading that had gone south, a real bad trip I'd had a few years earlier. I'd flown from Bangkok to Kolkata, having decided to spend the next six months or so wandering in India like some privileged and substance-abusing

mendicant. Before leaving Thailand, I bought a copy of An
Area of Darkness, *the first book in V.S. Naipaul's trilogy
about India. I read it on the plane – and immediately felt like
storming the cockpit and demanding that the pilot turn back.
So harsh and pessimistic was Naipaul's vision of India, it was
as if he wrote the book with the express intention of dissuading
anyone from ever setting foot in the place, especially not on
some Orientalist* Wanderjahr. *It's a curious sub-category of
travel writing, which we might label stay-at-home writing or
turn-back-now writing – the kind of book that persuades us
that a place is not worth visiting. A more positive variant of the
stay-at-home read is the kind that provides such a satisfying
virtual experience of a place that actually going there could
only be a disappointment. It's a way of thinking about literature
and travel that finds its purest expression in Huysmans's* À
rebours, *in which Des Esseintes gives up on going on journeys
in favour of reading about them instead:*

> *Travel, indeed, struck him as being a waste of time,
> since he believed that the imagination could provide a
> more-than-adequate substitute for the vulgar reality of
> actual experience.*

25 MICHEL HOUELLEBECQ

Whatever (1994)

Translated by Paul Hammond

In a text titled *Rester vivant* that was first published in French in 1991, Michel Houellebecq offers some advice to those pursuing the writer's vocation: 'All societies have their points of least resistance, their sore spots. Put your finger on the wound, and press down hard.' He also recommends hitting the bottle as you are 'tossed back and forth between bitterness and anguish', and milking the welfare state in order to thrive like a parasite 'upon the body of wealthy societies in a state of decay'. Decidedly, we are not in the noble halls of Marcus Aurelius or Seamus Heaney.

True to his word, Houellebecq has delivered multiple blows to society's solar plexus. He writes from a stronghold of abjection, where he has nothing to lose. While his masterpiece is *Atomised* – among the most distressingly original works of our times – his slim first novel is a superb declaration of hostilities. Published in English as *Whatever*, its original French title is more suggestive, translating as *The Extension of the Domain of the Struggle*.

Our narrator is a sexually frustrated chain-smoker with an office job. Reflecting bitterly on his inability to seduce women and the exhaustion of the age, he takes a work trip to the provinces with a gormless and unattractive colleague named Tisserand. After a series of humiliations at ugly discotheques, he encourages Tisserand to commit a racist murder to avenge his exclusion from the erotic paradise of the young and seductive.

Two decades before the emergence of the incels, the tech-amplified gender animosity and the current mood of sexual paranoia, Houellebecq brutally announced what may now be becoming apparent: we don't really want sexual liberation any more; it wasn't worth the cost. In his telling, we emerged from the cage, found ourselves at the mercy of the law of the jungle – the sexual free market – and now we'd rather go back inside and lock the door. With the lucidity of the depressed, Houellebecq's shattered narrator drives home the bitter message that the free-love generation were too naive to discern: 'Sexuality is a system of social hierarchy.'

Of the writers whose work I've loved, the only one I've ever seen cry is Michel Houellebecq. It was on French TV, the day after the terror attacks on the offices of Charlie Hebdo, *in which a cartoonist friend of Houellebecq's was among the victims. 'I've never known somebody who was assassinated before,' he told his interviewer, visibly rattled. An interesting account could perhaps be written of the years Houellebecq spent living in Ireland – a period that nourished his fiction, both in that he wrote some of his most important work here, and in that Ireland serves him as an occasional setting. I've heard various rumours and conjectures. For instance (and this seems fantastical to me), that he lived for a time in the undistinguished Dublin suburb of Lucan; also that he came here because he likes good Catholic girls (and not just to troll left-leaning literary France by abiding as a tax exile). The elegiac final section of* Atomised, *which unfolds in Clifden, County Galway, is as poetic as anything in Houellebecq. I recall one character's cursory description of Ireland as being a typical late twentieth-century European society, with its decline in religious belief, its proliferation of nightclubs and antidepressants. While living in Berlin I began writing a novel whose protagonist was a Houellebecq scholar. In my mind's eye the character looked like Houellebecq, and naturally he was burdened with classical Houellebecqian concerns, such as an imperilled libido and the bodies of nubile girls. I got about ten thousand words in before my interest dwindled. In an email, the author Rachel Kushner told me she is going to follow my suggestion and*

include Houellebecq as a character in the novel she's writing,
which apparently is set in France. The truth is I'm not even
sure I remember making such a suggestion, but if she doesn't
do it now I'll be disappointed.

Água Viva (1973)

Translated by Stefan Tobler

Some novelists dream of pruning the novel till it's all but bare. How much, they wonder, can I cut away, so that I'm not wasting the reader's time *approaching* what I want to say – elaborating plots and flicking characters into position like Subbuteo players – but simply *saying* it. Such novelists occasionally give up on the novel and become essayists. Others succeed in carving out heterodox, minimalist forms that replenish our understanding of what a novel can be. We might call such works the novels of subtraction. The late anti-novels of David Markson are emblematic of this category. So too is Fernando Pessoa's *The Book of Disquiet*.

Another writer who, like Pessoa, wrote in Portuguese – a language which has 'no bones', as Pessoa remarked – Clarice Lispector produced one work, erratic even in her own *oeuvre*, that must be counted among the noble failures in the literature of subtraction. Lispector was already a long-established novelist and short-story writer when, in 1966, she almost burned to death in her apartment in Rio de Janeiro. The accident left her disfigured, but she continued to write, and in 1973 she published *Água Viva*, which tells no story and contains no characters per se, only the voice of a woman – a painter – and the 'you' to whom she addresses her fervid, effusive thoughts.

Lispector had her doubts about *Água Viva*. 'I don't know why you liked my book,' she wrote to a friend before it was published. 'It's so bad, so bad, that I'm not going to publish it.' In one sense, she's right – it's bloody awful. The prose gushes with unfiltered emotion so that you don't know where to look. And yet, there is a thrill in reading these breathless, fitfully coherent fragments, each deployed in a vain quest to capture the living moment of naked existence, the 'now-instant'. *Água Viva* is an eccentric reminder, still useful at this late stage of the game, that the novel has nothing to lose but its chains.

The first winter I spent in Berlin, I moved into a vay-gay – *a W.G., meaning a shared apartment – on Kottbusser Strasse in Kreuzberg. I rented a room from a young Brazilian woman, a filmmaker, who was headed home for a few months. Unlike some of the rooms I've lived in, it was the kind of space you looked forward to getting back to – cosy, bright, full of plants. Its high windows looked out on the canal and the bridge, near to bars and* Spätis. *Even on nights in, when I lay on the couch to read, I could hear the hum of the city and feel I was not missing out. The shelves were lined with books in various languages about gender theory, film, contemporary art; books by Donna Haraway, Roberto Bolaño, Judith Butler. One of my flatmates was a trans woman who had published two novels in Swedish and was working on her first in English. She would wake late in the morning, laboriously arise and begin her day, sing in the shower. Afternoons she would ride the U-Bahn to the Staatsbibliothek library on Potsdamer Strasse and work until evening. Then she would come home, cook a huge meal of pasta to eat very late, and go to bed at maybe four in the morning. Sometimes we stayed up talking about books. She was devoted to Clarice Lispector –* Clarice-see *she called her, on first-name terms. She had read* Água Viva *many times, that being her favourite of Lispector's books, and had travelled to Brazil and visited the apartment in Rio de Janeiro where Lispector had lived. I think she even learned Portuguese so she could read her in the original. Later I moved across the river Spree, to Friedrichshain. Around Christmastime the following year, my former flatmate sent me her novel, asking for my thoughts before she sent it to publishers. When she came over to discuss it, I told her that the novel, which was autobiographical, caused me to remember something I'd once heard a psychoanalyst say: how it surprised him that more people with borderline personality disorder didn't commit suicide. She gestured towards the typescript, said that was the means by which she'd managed not to.*

27 SIGMUND FREUD

Civilisation and Its Discontents (1930)

Translated by David McLintock

If only we acted in accordance with our natures, our lives would pass in unrelenting massacre. We would howl in ecstasy as we eviscerated our foes, trampling their skulls and plunging our jaws into their innards to feast on gore, finally ripping out their hearts and raising them to the sky – until, all too quickly, a stronger party obliterated us. This much I'd figured out for myself early on, but only when I read Sigmund Freud did I find an honest theoretical acknowledgement of the unbridled aggression, depravity and lust for annihilation that constitute the dirtiest secret of the individual in society.

Freud has taken a kicking in the century since he revolutionised human self-understanding by methodically examining the 'seething cauldron' of unconscious motivation. To be sure, his conclusions tend towards the doctrinaire, his thought rooted in the nineteenth century's reductively mechanistic materialism. Nonetheless, in our times, Freud's dark vision of incorrigible human evil is a tonic to the obligatory optimism peddled by our overlords in Silicon Valley, and the reality-denialism of liberal ideology.

In his late work *Civilisation and Its Discontents*, Freud examines the neurosis he perceives as afflicting not only individuals, but entire cultures, possibly the entire species. We are born to an inheritance of aggression: in our pre-civilised state, we would gladly enslave the other, torturing and humiliating him for pleasure. Our relation to the world beyond our ego is one of enmity and hatred: we fear the other, knowing he is like us. 'Given this fundamental hostility of human beings to one another, civilised society is constantly threatened with disintegration.'

To preserve itself, civilisation imposes restraints on our natural instincts – and the psychic cost is immense. Painfully alienated from our repressed natures, we are tormented by guilt so that 'the price we pay for cultural progress is a loss of happiness'. As if that wasn't bad enough, beneath it all runs the 'death drive' – an ageless will to extinction inherent in organic life, and perhaps Freud's most divisive, suggestive, near-mythical notion.

With the world under lockdown, quarantine, stay-at-home orders – the terms vary but the basic experience being simultaneously had by everyone on the planet does not – there is talk of a widespread intensification of dream life. Across the globe, human beings report vivid or weird dreams, suggesting not a mass reckoning with Freudian sexual neurosis, but a disturbance in the collective unconscious whose existence was heretical to Freud. My own dreams have not been especially apocalyptic. A couple of nights ago, for instance, I dreamed of a girl we met in Berlin last summer. A little backstory here. It was one of our regular Saturday nights at KitKatClub, the extravagant techno-and-sex nightclub we had come to regard as the greatest party on earth. Out by the pool with the trapeze dangling above, languid bodies lay coiled together or poised expectantly amid a hum of chatter. Some were glowingly high; others emerged from the sauna to stand naked under the shower like trophies; others made love in twos or threes or more. We lay on a bed of cushions and together we stroked, kissed, caressed a brown-skinned young woman with sumptuous breasts. She told us she had broken up recently with her boyfriend, was still hurting, but was indulging her fantasies tonight. She described things she'd already done in the club's dark booths and rooms, or on the podium overlooking the main floor where hundreds of bodies throbbed to the euphoric beat. As she talked I began massaging my girlfriend's clit with the tips of two fingers, in circular motions that started slow and became faster as the two of them kissed, smiling and caressing one another's hair and cheeks. In time she began to come, while the other girl watched serenely, trailing a finger across her brow. After my girlfriend's orgasm subsided, the girl told us her Instagram handle, and the next day we followed her and she followed us back. We never met her again, though we fantasised sometimes about a sequel, languorously spending a whole night with her, all of us taking our time, drawing it out. The photos on her Instagram portrayed a happy life of friendship, laughter, youth. As the months passed, this portal onto the girl's world took on for me a bittersweet quality, coming to represent the realm I was being drawn mercilessly away from – a realm of endless sexual possibility, the body exulting in itself and universally desired – towards a sterile and cold reality. And now I'm in this coastal town that's far in every way from the Berlin night. It seems possible that the city's orgiastic clubs will never open again, all those bodies heaving together in an abandon of proximity. The other night, when I dreamed of the girl whose body we kissed and stroked by the pool, it was not straightforwardly a dream of regret or sexual longing. Although she was dressed in a revealing outfit of the kind that would fit right in at KitKat, and though we explored together a nightclub very much like it, the rapport between us was one of cordiality rather than lust. We parted on easy terms, smiling affectionately. I wonder if the dream really does mean what I took it to mean on waking: that I'm making my peace with the transition to a new phase of life, maturer and less desirous, with an attendant advancement in my relation to the feminine. But maybe that's not it. Maybe it's that the unconscious too is being surveilled and censored, and even when we dream we stay woke – the Id and the Shadow eager to show that their problematic urges have been tamed.

118

In this paradigm, the dream can be read as an endorsement of my rehabilitation, a plea of good behaviour to the parole board of a culture demanding total virtue and good clean living. The evening after I'd had the dream, reflecting on how Berlin's sex-party scene is being hammered by Covid-19, I wrote a post I found amusing. After a moment's consideration, I deleted it, because it seemed to me that people might miss the joke, because it wasn't entirely a joke, and that this sincerity hidden in plain sight was in fact the non-joke's unfunny essence. It went something like:

> If there's a silver lining to all this, it's that the new generation won't get to enjoy the freedoms I made such a beast of myself exploiting.

28 TERENCE MCKENNA

The Archaic Revival (1991)

Terence McKenna, the most original spokesperson for the psychedelic experience since hallucinogens swept through Western culture less than a century ago, is an either/or thinker. One either finds him fascinating, or dismisses him as a peddler of irresponsible nonsense. Where you come down on the divide will depend to a large degree on whether you have had or are interested in having a full-blown psychedelic experience: a 40mg hit of DMT, say, or what McKenna calls a 'heroic dose' of psilocybin mushrooms. Let me put my cards on the table: McKenna's speculative ideas are so drastic, novel and astounding in their possible implications, that I sometimes imagine future ages regarding him the way we do Copernicus.

A superb introduction to his work, *The Archaic Revival* is a collection of essays, talks and interviews in which these ideas gush forth in a face-melting cascade (no less vital are audio recordings of McKenna's wildly entertaining public talks, many hours of which are available on YouTube). For McKenna – who refused the guru role, urging verification by direct experience – psychedelics are a supercharged shamanic technology that bring us face to face with the absolute Other: 'Right here and now, one quanta away, there is a raging universe of active intelligence that is transhuman, hyperdimensional, and extremely alien.' In a relatively sober essay, McKenna proposes a theory of human evolution in which consciousness developed in symbiosis with the mysterious intelligence within magic mushrooms (and these – it's getting loopy now – may be a technology of interstellar communication).

A splendidly eloquent polymath, McKenna is at his best when extemporising: the interview and lecture formats suit him well. Whenever his ideas career towards stoner lunacy, his lively wit reassures us that he hasn't lost his mind. Even in a chapter about sex with aliens, the speculations are thoughtful and poignant. Perhaps the persistent UFO sightings in our consumerist civilisation, McKenna suggests, emanate from the collective unconscious, and indicate a grave alienation from our own enigmatic depths. In which case, loving the alien would mean rediscovering ourselves.

There was alcohol, to begin with; there were cigarettes. There was the thought, on first getting drunk at age fifteen: 'I want to feel this way all the time.' There was cannabis – hash, then weed. There was the psychosis it triggered: a gradual darkening, then three years in hell. There were poppers. There was ecstasy and amphetamine. There were powders, pills, liquids, shards. There were psilocybin mushrooms. There was MDMA. There were comedowns, withdrawals. There was cocaine, and a basement bar in La Paz where waitresses served it on silver trays with fluorescent straws. There was mescaline. There was opium, in a wooden house on stilts in Laos. There was tolerance. There was LSD, the first time on a Thai island at a psy-trance rave. There was ketamine. There was diazepam, bought over the counter in distant countries, and later on prescription. There was the San Pedro cactus, while camping in the canyons outside Tupiza with some local slackers. There was the gunky ayahuasca brew. There was mephedrone, which made social life turn menacing. There were legal highs whose names I've forgotten or never knew. There was codeine. There was modafinil. There was insufflation, vaporising, dissolving under the tongue. There was microdosing. There was never injecting. There was Lyrica. There was propranolol hydrochloride. There was tramadol. There was DMT, which a girlfriend went on to manufacture. There was Viagra. There was Seroquel. There was Klonopin, mirtazapine, amitriptyline, lorazepam – benzos sponged from women on Tinder dates or swapped with friends. There was Xanax. There was sertraline.

29 THOMAS BERNHARD

Woodcutters (1985)

Translated by David McLintock

All of Thomas Bernhard's novels are the same, except that some of them are better than others, and some, like *Yes* or *Wittgenstein's Nephew*, shorter. So let's choose *Woodcutters*, as enjoyable a showcase as any for Bernhard's thrillingly maniacal prose style.

The ingredients in the Bernhard soufflé are as follows: caustic and unremitting misanthropy; long, obsessive, involuted sentences that generate a techno-like intensity; paragraphs so huge and airless that they take up a whole book. Among the targets of Bernhard's inexhaustible derision are other people, Austria, intellectual weakness and almost everything else. In *Woodcutters*, we trace the bilious thoughts of a Viennese bourgeois at a midnight dinner party following a performance of an Ibsen play. The narrator spends the first half of the novel in a 'wing chair', holding a glass of champagne and silently taking the piss out of everything he sees. In the second half, a lauded actor arrives and the dinner unfolds. The pretensions of the Viennese cultural set are mocked pitilessly. The sycophancy, social climbing and cravenness that infest the arts scene are spared no insult. Bernhard made enemies with this novel. Fair enough: if you recognised yourself in one of the lampooned characters, you would want to pick up the author in his wing chair and hurl him from a high window.

Bernhard's literary project was a locomotive fuelled by spleen. Life disgusted him. This might be merely annoying, like the moping of the heavy metal fan at school, if it were not for Bernhard's funniness. As his sentences pile up with qualifications and reversals and repetitions, they combust into hilarity. You may still occasionally feel like smacking the author around the head for his faux-profundity and supercilious cynicism. But don't smack him too hard, because without Bernhard there would be no W.G. Sebald (or not as we know him), and no Geoff Dyer when he draws deranging comedy from the centrifugal blur of his neurosis. In Bernhard, the howl of laughter and the scream of despair are one.

Bernhard published a short book titled My Prizes, *which collects the acerbic speeches he gave on receiving various literary awards. I'm thinking of writing a similarly titled book, of acerbic speeches to mark the literary prizes I did* not *win, which at the time of writing is quite a lot of them, all of them in fact. Being overlooked for literary prizes in favour of writers you secretly deem inferior – in the way that all writers secretly deem all their peers inferior – tends to provoke a reflexive inversion of valuations: you tell yourself you failed to win the prize not in spite of your book's greater worth than whatever dumb people-pleaser stirred the mob, but because of it. Thus, ergo, QED: the reason you didn't win the prize was because you deserved it more than the others. So in a way, you did win! And if even after such slinky dialectics your ego is still bruised, you can turn for support to fellow losers who likewise saw through the problematic, not to say entirely fraudulent business of handing out literary 'prizes'. Will Self jibed somewhere or other that 'only pets win prizes'. Roberto Bolaño, patron saint of writers who dangle over the pit of oblivion and usually fall in, wrote with characteristic waywardness that 'literature has nothing to do with national prizes and everything to do with a strange rain of blood, sweat, semen and tears', with prizes reserved for those 'who play the part of loyal and obedient clerks'. That's reassuring, amid the hangover that follows another awards ceremony where you watched some schmoozing chump win the latest popularity contest with her bullshit book. Yes, it's possible to arm yourself with an arsenal of such ripostes, and*

127

*each time a dopey grinning rival is handed another trophy of
the public's esteem along with a cheque for several thousand
euro, you can skulk off into a shady corner and intone them
to yourself.*

SCUM Manifesto (1968)

For a man, Valerie Solanas's notorious *SCUM Manifesto* pro-
vokes the same kind of alarmed interest as jihadi magazines
like *Dabiq* or *Inspire* – the frisson of seeing oneself through
the eyes of those who will one's extermination. While *SCUM* –
'Society for Cutting Up Men' – fulfils all the requirements
for hate speech, it differs from the likes of Anders Breivik's
manifesto or Adolf Hitler's *Mein Kampf* not only by its occasional funniness, but by Solanas's relative ineptitude as a
terrorist or despot. When she took her war against men to
the streets, the bullet she fired into Andy Warhol's chest (he
'refused to pay attention to me') failed to kill him, though it
left him traumatised for life.

The reference to Hitler is not entirely below the belt.
Solanas writes about men the way Hitler did about Jews or
the way ISIS fighters do about 'infidels': 'The elimination of
any male is, therefore, a righteous and good act.' She even
advocates eugenics: 'When genetic control is possible – and
soon it will be – it goes without saying that we should produce only whole, complete beings, not physical defects or
deficiencies... such as maleness.'

To do away with the existing order, Solanas proposes a sort
of feminazi Fight Club, whereby agents of SCUM 'become
members of the unwork force, the fuck-up force; they will get
jobs of various kinds and unwork'. Some of her slurs had my
ears burning: 'The male likes death – it excites him sexually

and, already dead inside, he wants to die', but my feelings got hurt when she described me and my bros as 'walking abortions' and 'walking dildos' in the space of two pages.

I propose an alternative way to read this scary book: wherever Solanas writes 'the male' or 'men', read instead 'Valerie Solanas'. The hate thus converts back to its basic poignancy, the rage to pain. Victim–criminal of a fucked-up world, Solanas/the male lived 'trapped inside himself, incapable of empathising or identifying with others, of love, friendship, affection, of tenderness. He is a completely isolated unit'.

Have you ever been hated – truly hated? And have you ever hated anyone? Not for a hot flash but sustainedly, a scorching murderous hatred where every day for months or years you visualise torturing, mutilating, eviscerating the target of your hate, kicking their skull in, mangling their genitals, gouging their eyeballs out? It seems to me that if we answer at least the second of these questions in the affirmative, we have failed some important test as human beings. I didn't always see it. I was so accustomed to construing life as warfare that I assumed hate like I felt it was universal. Various women have told me they don't have it in them to hate like I do. I've been drawn to these women, felt safe with them, felt that they were better than me and that loving them would make me better too, and it did. I've encountered other women whose hate was as violent and bitter as mine, who were made ugly by hate. I've been drawn to some of these women too, in an attraction whose end point was always carnage and torture. I read in a biography of Nietzsche that it was only when he was rejected by Lou Andreas-Salomé that he first knew what it was to hate someone. He took revenge on her, and afterwards he was ashamed of his pettiness. He recognised that hatred had lowered him, sapped his dignity. In the final interview he gave in his lifetime, Roberto Bolaño was asked whether he hated anybody. He replied that he had never felt true hatred, only moments of anger that soon passed. You can sense it in the work, I think. Reading of such people who pass through life without hating, I feel sullied beyond redemption. I expect I'll be paying off the hatred I've permitted,

I've wallowed in, for the rest of my days. In Buddhist thinking, hatred is the inner state regarded as the most dangerous, the one to be resisted with extreme urgency, the creator of hells. But there is also a Buddhist maxim, attributed to Padmasambhava, originator of the *Bardo Thodol*, in which I can take comfort even with the flames licking my flesh. Padmasambhava said, 'Hell is the lama of all the Buddhas.'

31 ANDRÉ BRETON

Nadja (1928)

Translated by Richard Howard

Nadja may not be a *great* book, but it is a strange and unique one. Is it a novel? Not really. Or rather, yes, but in the attractive French sense in which pretty much anything can be called a novel (the French have no need for such generic ghettos as 'creative non-fiction'). André Breton's *Nadja* is the leader of the surrealist movement's story of his enchantment with a liminal, odd young woman who seems to him the living embodiment of surrealism. By the end of the book, these qualities have landed Nadja in the mental asylum, which gives Breton a chance to fume about the psychiatric profession – 'They shut up Sade, they shut up Nietzsche; they shut up Baudelaire' – before abandoning Nadja in order to write about her.

Avant-garde trailblazer though he was, Breton does come across a bit insufferable. He talks pompously at the object of his fascination, and occasionally hectors the reader too ('Anyone who laughs at this last sentence is a pig'). What makes *Nadja* interesting, though, is Breton's keen sense of mystery and magic, and the plausibility-stretching coincidences he recounts. Nadja appears to him almost as an emissary from some non-terrestrial plane, a being freed from the 'hateful prison' of logic and alert to numinous transmissions.

There is a certain type of reader – me – who will read books simply because they are set in certain cities: Paris,

Tokyo, Berlin. The mystique of street names is sustenance enough even in pages heavy with indifferent plots – not that there is any plot to speak of in this instance. Among other things, *Nadja* is a whirl through the squares and boulevards of a Paris that was still, as Nietzsche had put it a few decades earlier, the only city in Europe for artists.

Breton is into digressions. He fulminates against boring jobs – 'There is no use being alive if one must work' – and against the boring novels that the surrealist movement naively believed it would do away with – 'Happily the days of psychological literature, with all its fictitious plots, are numbered.'

Speaking of books we read so as to mainline the satisfactions of place, a writer I regret not including in this round-up, in part to avoid committing the sin of obviousness, is Jack Kerouac. It's true he falls into the irksome category of writers who win approval from people who rarely read books, but let's hate the game and not the player, because for all his teenage girl's effusiveness ('as sentimental as a lollipop,' jibed Norman Mailer), his lack of reserve that made him once so radical and now canonically uncool, Kerouac played a blinder – not least when he wrote The Dharma Bums, *of which I so wish I had a copy here in my book-rationed quarantine. In literature as in cinema, I don't really want stuffy rooms or offices, I want mountain peaks with bracing air, deep clear lakes, forests and gullies, coasts and deserts and the highways that streak across them, all the way to cities of the plain or the cities of the red night. In short, I want the landscapes of America, and I want Jack Kerouac to lead me through them, breathlessly ecstatic and less than reasonable. And even if, in the end, 'the only thing to do is sit in a room and get drunk', as Kerouac wrote through a mist of tears before dying of a failed liver at the age of forty-seven; even if it dawns on us too late that we're on the road to nowhere, the road to ruin, and that Kerouac's America and its landscapes are long gone, sucked up and rendered as saleable data; even if the promise of the open road turns out to be as empty as the dream of a utopian internet, and none of it will ever be great again, I'll still have been thankful for the joyride.*

Writing on Drugs (1999)

Myths are fun, they enrich life, and the Cybernetic Culture Research Unit (Ccru) that emerged at University of Warwick in the mid-nineties, and briefly threatened to upend all academic and philosophical orthodoxies in a riot of Jungle music and incendiary rhetoric, is an irresistible subject for mythologising. The Ccru was a renegade thought-collective whose enduring theoretical innovation was acceleration-ism – a glamorously dangerous political orientation that, despite the 'left' or 'right' colourings it is often lent, is at core a submission to nihilistic *jouissance*: getting off on the race towards a post-human catastrophe wherein all prior certainties vanish.

Among the Ccru's chief agitators were the unsettlingly immoderate Nick Land, who once suggested he was an android sent back from the future to undermine human security, and would offer his students such helpful advice as, 'Think of life as an open wound, which you poke with a stick to amuse yourself'; Mark Fisher, who went on to produce brilliantly fertile cultural criticism until his suicide in 2017; and Sadie Plant, a once-lauded writer who has fallen into obscurity since the turn of the millennium.

Having established herself with a book on the Situationist International and another on 'digital women and the new tech-noculture', Plant wrote an impressive study of the immense role drugs have played in shaping Western civilisation, from science and technology to literature and warfare. While there have been some notable additions to the narco-bookshelf in recent decades, *Writing on Drugs* is among the few written by a woman: indeed, Plant suggests that drugs may not be such a big deal for women, who 'have a pre-existing sympathy for the worlds their male counterparts explore on drugs'.

Underpinning *Writing on Drugs* is Plant's conviction that any 'war on drugs' is a pointless absurdity. Drug users who bring weird news from inner space have always replenished mainstream culture. Besides, there's nothing more human than craving temporary escape from the brutal skull-hotel of consciousness – what Nick Land, before his acceleration into seriously ugly politics, called the 'headcase'.

One Saturday in Dublin I led a workshop in writing non-fiction, a few floors up a Georgian building on Parnell Square that looked onto the Garden of Remembrance. I gave the participants photocopied texts to read and discuss, among them a section from Mark Fisher's Ghosts of My Life, and the first few pages of Édouard Levé's singular Autoportrait. One of the participants remarked on the preponderance among my selection of authors who had committed suicide. In reply I told the group about the creative writing classes the philosopher Simon Critchley ran in New York devoted to the suicide note. Together with his students, Critchley analysed as literature the notes of famous suicides, from Kurt Cobain to Hunter S. Thompson (the latter's was praised for its economy of style). Critchley wrote about these classes in his book Notes On Suicide, which he commences by admitting to his own suicidal fantasies – the book is an investigation into an act that is also that act's deferral (and thus a double-barrelled instantiation of Cioran's dictum that 'A book is a suicide postponed'). I don't know whether Mark Fisher left a note when he committed suicide in January 2017, weeks after the publication of his final book, The Weird and the Eerie. I heard about his death via a late-night text from a friend who had previously interviewed Fisher. She was badly disturbed, having looked to his work for insights to navigate her own fraught place in the world (I had in fact come to Fisher's books through her). Later, I would find myself dwelling on the timing of Fisher's suicide, so soon after his book was published. At the time of Fisher's death I was writing a book that had consumed my creative energies for several years – and racked, for the first time in my life, with serious and compulsive thoughts of suicide. As the end of the project drew closer, this death wish gave way to anxiety that I would die. With a few chapters to go, I began to fear taking flights because if the plane crashed the book would never be finished. I worried that cars I was in would veer off the road, or that I would be killed in a terror attack. When I projected myself forward to a point in time after the book's publication, such fears dissolved – whether I lived or died once the book existed seemed unimportant. Here and now, on the other side, with the book I was writing then safely out in the world, I feel invested again in my own continued existence, which is a vessel to carry the present book into being. I expect it will continue in such a manner till there is more life and more books behind me than there are up ahead, and I can look back over it all, rueing every moment I spent wanting it to end.

33 *Dhammapada* (estimated first century BC)

Translated by Jack Austin

Cosmic spoiler alert: life is suffering. Thrown into a bewildering existence, we swing between the flames of agony and relief in fleeting pleasures, until old age and sickness finish us off. The *Dhammapada*, one of the canonical scriptures of Theravada Buddhism and a text that remains as relevant as anything that scrolls down our social media feeds, urges that it need not be this way. In 423 aphorisms aimed at the roots of human distress, it promises nothing less than the path to the cessation of suffering, or nirvana.

Buddhism has held an abiding appeal to Westerners since it was introduced to our civilisation some two centuries ago. Instead of a faith-based belief system, it provides a rational framework of mental cultivation well suited to post-Enlightenment scepticism towards revealed religion and divine authority. Moreover, Buddhism posits a world that is fundamentally moral: good, thoughtful actions will be rewarded by inner peace, and evil, thoughtless ones will bring about the 'hell states' that afflict the cruel and unrighteous. 'Even a wrongdoer is happy so long as his evil has not ripened; but when it bears its fruit he suffers.'

The aphorisms of the *Dhammapada* gain force from all that stands unsaid around them: the elegant Buddhist and Hindu metaphysics of *anatta* (non-self) and *anicca* (impermanence). Consider aphorism 3: '"He reviled me, struck me, defeated me, robbed me." In those who harbour such thoughts hatred will never cease.' A blow is a blow, but we needlessly torture ourselves if we believe in the separate existence of a self on which these apparent wrongs have been inflicted. To disengage from the ego is to pour cool water on the red-hot coals of the psyche.

So can this 2,000 year-old text really offer relief to twenty-first century Western neurosis? Yes, it can: it's hard to live up to its ethical precepts, but even floundering efforts in that direction pay off. As Nietzsche remarked on the thought of suicide, by means of the *Dhammapada* one can get through many a bad night.

In Thailand I went on several meditation retreats in Buddhist monasteries. During the longest of these, one of the few times I broke the code of silence was to speak with an Englishman who had been ordained and was living there as a monk, draped in his saffron robe. Eager to talk, he gushed out his story to me, and a few years later I wrote it down, in the first person, as a short story that I reworked for quite a few months before abandoning it. Phra Tim, as I named him in the story, and which may even have been his name in real life, had worked in the City of London after finishing college. It was what was expected of him, he said, the way a bullet is inserted into the chamber of a gun and fired. It was high-pressure, Wolf of Wall Street stuff, and at weekends he drank copiously and chased skirt. Thus unfurled his mid-twenties, until finally he cracked. Enduring a breakdown, he quit work and flew to Thailand for three months of debauchery on the beaches. In the midst of the drinking and shagging, he caught a few arresting glimpses of Buddhism, meditation, the path of Oriental wisdom. Back in England, he retreated to his family's large country home. There he began reading Eastern philosophy, starting with the basics and progressing to more rarefied texts. He began to discern a marketing opportunity: there were lots of maddened Westerners like him, in dire need of the calm and insight he was discovering through dharmic teachings. Deciding he needed to gain credentials, he flew back to South East Asia, this time to spend an indefinite period studying at various monasteries. In Bangkok, he decided he would go all-in and train as a monk, the better to impress potential clients when he started his Meditation for Traders business back home. Initially he figured he'd fold up his robe after a year or so, but when I met him he was three years in, and no longer sure he wanted to teach Buddhist wisdom to coke-snorting executives. 'They keep smashing their heads against the wall,' he told me, 'and they want to deal with it by taking paracetamol. You can't get it through to them that they're going to have to stop banging their heads against the wall.' I ended my short story with Phra Tim being tempted away from the monkhood after a pretty Westerner visits the monastery, wandering the grounds in loose white garments. In reality, he might be anywhere.

34 MILAN KUNDERA

The Art of the Novel (1986)

Translated by Linda Asher

In the great novels of Milan Kundera's middle period – *The Book of Laughter and Forgetting*, *The Unbearable Lightness of Being* and *Immortality* – fiction and playful philosophical reflection merge in a form of marvellous elegance and compression; a uniquely novelistic kind of essay unfurls in counterpoint to narrative. With these books, something new happened in literature. The best part is that Kundera's avant-garde genius precluded neither popularity nor readability. He mastered a modernist reboot of the novel with none of the aristocratic disdain for the reader cultivated by high modernists earlier in the twentieth century. I've known people who hardly read any fiction but devour Kundera.

The first of his non-fiction books, *The Art of the Novel* is a seven-part essay that is 'no theoretical statement at all' but rather 'a practitioner's confession' – a guide to Kundera's conception of the history of the novel as it is embodied in his own work.

By the novel, Kundera specifically means the European novel, beginning with Cervantes and Rabelais and encompassing all those practitioners who have carried forth the spirit of this art form, which to Kundera is the spirit of the modern era itself. Kundera's avid Europhilia is especially stirring now that the integrity of Europe is imperilled once again. He wants us to realise that over some five centuries, a treasure without equal has been cultivated here – and what a loss it will be if we allow it to disintegrate.

Fittingly, Kundera is a stern defender of the 'great European art' he practised: 'A novel that does not uncover a hitherto unknown segment of existence is immoral. Knowledge is the novel's only morality.' He celebrates the novel's spirit of complexity, irony and moral ambiguity, and calls for an art of 'radical divestment' – that is, for novelists to pare away as much superfluity as possible and 'always head straight for the heart of things'. Fellow practitioners could do worse than to write by Kundera's core maxim: 'The novel's sole *raison d'être* is to say what only the novel can say.'

AUTOBIOGRAPHY: *In a section of* The Art of the Novel *titled 'Sixty-Three Words', wherein Kundera lists the words and ideas that mean most to him, he deplores the modern drift towards interest in the life of the author, which threatens to supplant interest in the works. In the twenty-first century, however, the life and the work are collapsing into one another, just as the public and interior selves have merged in a diffused and transparent mode of selfhood. There is no longer as much drive as there once was to construct fictitious realities and illusions of character. The tendency rather is to channel imagination into framing and aestheticising the real. The historical role of fiction having been pretty much fulfilled, the novel as a cultural form seems to lose its lustre, and so we try to leave it behind – and in this way it survives, is remade, stays novel.*

DEATH: *'In contemporary Western society,' writes Michel Houellebecq, 'death is like white noise to a man in good health; it fills his mind when his dreams and plans fade. With age, the noise becomes increasingly insistent, like a dull roar with the occasional screech. In another age the sound meant waiting for the kingdom of God; it is now an anticipation of death.' I first read that as a teenager and had no reason to disbelieve it. Perhaps it means only that I can't withstand as much reality as I once could, but almost two decades on I'm less convinced that such stark certainties amount to a final word. Houellebecq's declaration looks to me now like the summation of the twentieth-century ontological nihilism of which he was* the terminal proponent. Today that sort of bulletproof atheism is harder to pull off. Science and religion used to be regarded as adversaries, but as we become more keenly aware of reality's confounding weirdness, science and religion seem poised to blur together on an event horizon of the quantum sublime. What is being revealed amid all the astrophysical speculation isn't necessarily the good news. I've felt now and then, from my stoned and spooked layman's balcony over the abyss, that the uncanny vistas opened by theoretical physics and all that stuff are so disconcerting to human suppositions, so warping of our sense of ourselves and our cherished beliefs, that we might come to regard this body of knowledge as evil – a forbidden gnosis, a satanic revelation. As we uncover more, perhaps the notion of death as the white noise of cessation will come even to seem a merciful illusion, a salvation.

FUCKING: The gerund is an ugly one, crude and brutal, devoid of sensuality. So what are we supposed to call it? Making love? I often want to, but fear being thought sentimental. Having sex? It sounds so… gynaecological. The slang terms are likewise anti-erotic, dismal, off-putting, like calling the striploin steak on your plate a slab of cow. A quandary facing not only writers but all of us alive in these fucking times: what to call it?

JAPAN: A place I've never visited, imbued in my fantasies with mystique and fascination. Each of us, perhaps, holds the idea of such a place, the one we long to see more than anywhere else – and for this reason we should avoid ever going there. It thus remains a zone of desire and enigma, a space on the map onto which we project our capacity for enchantment.

PUNK: *Not as a fixed aesthetic, still less a musical style, but a mode of being, a style of perception that pre-existed the cultural movement that gave it its name and rendered it visible in the world. Perhaps, beyond that, a cosmic principle that has always been and always will be, which manifests on earth in phenomena as various as the wandering mendicant, the obscene gestures of Diogenes the Cynic, the girl who studies hardest, rappers with face tattoos, Shylock, the romantic in a city of cynics.*

PROBLEMATIC: *A judgement generated by the demand that art avoid describing what is and express what ought to be, and that we admire only art that issues from a stainless soul and a clean rap sheet. Everything in the human being that is messy, vital and interesting; everything shadowy, unconscious, offline.*

THREESOME: *In each era a particular sexual act becomes the locus of male fantasy. Discussing the fixation on fellatio in the work of a certain superannuated novelist, a friend dismissively remarked, 'That's a seventies fixation.' The three-way fulfils the role in the early decades of the twenty-first century that fellatio used to. Like the blowjob, the act (or the fantasy of it) is bound up with masculine ego. As with the blowjob, this element of egoism, while making the fantasy exciting to men, also makes it distressing (when they imagine other men enjoying it; when they are excluded from it). The three-way is a contemporary apparatus for reminding us of the awkward persistence, post-sexual liberation, of sex's indivisibility from questions of rank.*

35 EMMANUEL CARRÈRE

The Adversary (2000)

Translated by Linda Coverdale

Emmanuel Carrère had been writing books for almost two decades when he published *The Adversary*, the intense true-crime work that commenced one of the more fascinating literary projects of our times: Carrère's sequence of 'non-fiction novels' that also includes *My Life as a Russian Novel*, *Lives Other Than My Own, Limonov* and *The Kingdom*. In these post-fictional works, Carrère puts himself front and centre, incorporating his struggle to write each book as a narrative element within it. This is no dry academic pursuit like that of the American postmodernists who were in vogue a few decades earlier, but a gripping new mode of narration whereby the author declines to pretend he is an invisible witness and reveals the blood on his hands. Nor was Carrère motivated by that jadedness with the process of fictionalisation that has led the likes of Karl Ove Knausgaard or Rachel Cusk to seek new trails in autobiographical writing: by his own admission, Carrère still wanted to write novels, he just couldn't do it any more.

In 1993, Carrère began a correspondence with Jean-Claude Romand, who was awaiting trial for having murdered his wife, parents and children after cracks had begun to show in the elaborate lie he'd been living for decades, involving a non-existent career in the World Health Organisation, and money borrowed in secret desperation to maintain the trappings of bourgeois normality. In *The Adversary*, Carrère finds himself identifying unsettlingly with Romand, seeing himself reflected in the abyss of Romand's shame and the horror its exposure unleashed.

Indeed, there is a monstrous vanity at the core of Carrère's project – the kind of vanity that entails exhibiting the most odious and tortured corners of one's psyche. Ever since *The Adversary*, even when he is telling the story of early Christianity as a PKD-style thriller of metaphysical insurrection (*The Kingdom*), or narrating the astounding life of a volatile Russian author (*Limonov*), Emmanuel Carrère has been writing primarily about himself. Because he does it so brilliantly, you wouldn't want it any other way.

There is a hashtag going around marking pictures in which people show off their bookshelves. My own books are, if not scattered on the four winds, at least diffused across a number of addresses. Because of the questionable decisions I've made in life, unlike many men my age I do not own a home of my own, but still drift between temporary addresses, staying a few months and then moving on. Consequently, the important question of where my books should reside has never been resolved. Some of them are here, in the house in Wexford where I'm waiting out the pandemic. Others are in the flat I rent in Berlin, where I was due to move back right about now, before the airline fleets were grounded and the borders tightened. Most of my books are at my parents' house in Dublin, the house I grew up in – a fact I record with a touch of shame. If it weren't for my books I'd be as light as air, unburdened by much in the way of earthly possessions. A minority part of me would like to be done with them, just drift on the breeze. To promote my most recent book I made a short film with the help of some friends, in which a pile of my own books is ceremonially burned by three figures in ski masks. We filmed on a secluded hillside near Phoenix Park. All dressed in black, three friends ignited the pyre we'd doused with lighter fluid, and stood in a menacing formation as it all went up in a gratifying blaze, which I shot on my phone. In our first edit, we set the film to an Islamic nasheed played backwards. It was sinister and confrontational, a desert-snuff-film flashback spliced with Troubles-era sectarian tropes. In the end we changed the soundtrack to a chorus of throat-singing Tibetan monks, likewise played backwards, having ruefully decided that the flagrant homage to jihadist murder aesthetics would risk the video overshadowing the book it was intended to boost. I timed the video to go out on my social media channels at the exact time of the book's official launch, captioned with a text from a 1980s serial killer film. People didn't seem to know what to make of it.

36 STEFAN AUST

The Baader-Meinhof Complex (1985)

Translated by Anthea Bell

This terrific book by the long-time editor of *Der Spiegel* magazine, Stefan Aust, was turned into a gripping 2008 film which made the trail of mayhem wreaked by the terrorist Red Army Faction in the 1970s seem rather sexy. Clad in a short skirt, Gudrun Ensslin cradles a sub-machine gun between her suggestively parted legs, and says, 'Screwing and shooting are the same.'

This collision of post-sixties Dionysianism, radical chic and anti-authoritarianism was indeed crucial to the emergence of the RAF, which waged guerrilla war on what its members believed was a resurgent fascism within the German state. As Aust's unflinching book shows, however, the reality was more grim and sordid. By the end of *The Baader-Meinhof Complex*, it's impossible to feel much sympathy for the charismatic Andreas Baader and the damaged, middle-class acolytes he led on a campaign of bombing, shooting, arson and kidnapping. The curious titular word choice comes to seem apt: the RAF was pathological.

Ulrike Meinhof was an establishment journalist who, radicalised during protests against the Vietnam War, crossed a line of no return by assisting in the escape from prison of Andreas Baader. From then on, she becomes the intellectual mouthpiece of the group (her underground writings were later published as *Everybody Talks About the Weather...*

We Don't). They move around Europe, rob banks and plan attacks, and receive combat training in the Middle East. A massive manhunt ends in 1972 with the capture of the group's leaders.

It is at this point that sympathy begins to dwindle. During a lengthy trial, RAF supporters on the outside resort to brutal means to secure the group's release. It's no longer about world revolution: it's about them. A passenger plane is hijacked; innocent people are slain. Ulrike Meinhof hangs herself in her cell. Ultimately, the Red Army Faction fall prey to a danger faced by all revolutionaries: they murder their humanity in the name of humanitarian ideals. The morning after another failed bid for release, the ringleaders are all found dead in their cells.

Missing from this survey of the books that helped shape me is a book that was written in prison. I ought to have included, say, Genet's Our Lady of the Flowers, *or* Soul on Ice *by the Black Panther radical Eldridge Cleaver, which I read as a student and whose violence and intensity made me feel I was holding in my hands something dangerous. As I write this page, more than half of the world's population is virtually incarcerated in their homes. Naturally, writers are doing relatively okay in this new indoor world, a paradise of the introverts. I've broken quarantine once – to ride an empty train up the coast to Dublin on an amatory visit, fibbing to the conductor that I had to see my doctor – but otherwise the solitude has been total. At first I felt smug satisfaction at how the whole planet was being forced to live like I do, my lifestyle suddenly in the spotlight. But as the weeks wore on, it dawned on me that that lifestyle – the screen-fixated, cocooning, non-essential life of the writer in the twenty-first century – was already a nadir of the mode of being endemic to Western modernity. Even though, in the first months of this year, everything changed, in a sense nothing changed at all – it just became more of itself. If the grandkids I'll never have were to ask me, 'What did you do during the great lockdown of 2020?', I'll answer that I did what I'd done before the lockdown: I gazed at my phone; I streamed content; I scrolled the feed; I flirted with people I expected never to meet; I refreshed. It isn't new, this conjuring of an absent community through phantom substitutes, the content less important than the ritual of its shared consumption. It's comforting to know*

157

we're bingeing the same series as everyone else, at the same time. 'I'm late to the party,' begin posts about books published just a few months earlier (I should have titled this book about the literary past I'm Late to the Party). Certain experiences, though, have changed. In the early days of lockdown, I idly watched a certain amount of porn. However, with no erotic life beyond itself for porn to gesture towards, I experienced a sort of peering behind the scenery. The inner mechanism was laid bare. In a newly static world, the trick failed – not just the trick of pornography, but of sex itself. It was as if while watching the lesbians and orgies I could perceive the blind maw of insatiable craving, the desire whose transient salving masks the reality of infinite disappointment. Arousal depends on a degree of entrancement, an inspired state. But these bodies that slapped and ground together were meat-models stripped of their aura, the charisma of desirability. Watching Pornhub felt like a nightmarish roam through an infinite wet market, such as those in Wuhan where some claim the virus originated. As I compulsively watched, wondering if I'd ever be aroused again, a more hopeful intuition emerged from the unease: namely, that this experience of revulsion at the raw truth of sex was a kernel of liberation. My desirelessness, brought on by a rupture in the circuitry of craving and gratification, permitted me a moksha-like glimpse of the cessation of all lust. I'm still feeling a bit creaky, a bit self-disgusted. It will pass. I'll wake up tomorrow and walk along the cliffs, remind myself I'm a corporeal being and not just a node in a vector of commerce and data. I hope never to see the inside of a prison, but if it came to it, I know I'd do okay in some basic sense at least. Distractions would fall away. I wouldn't be able to impose redundant obligations on myself or allow others to impose them on me. I might even weep in the dark of my cell at night, sorry for my sad entire life, but boredom would not be much of an issue, and regret makes words blaze on the page.

*Vulgar Favours: Andrew Cunanan,
Gianni Versace, and the Largest Failed
Manhunt in U.S. History* (1999)

The most upsetting and unexpectedly profound art experience I've had lately was watching the 2018 TV series *The
Assassination of Gianni Versace*. A riveting study in shame,
self-loathing and damnation, the series set itself an audacious
narrative and moral challenge: it began *in medias res* with the
preppy, erudite serial killer Andrew Cunanan committing
acts so repugnantly vicious they put him beyond any hope
of redemption, and then, by way of a slow-burning reverse
chronology, lured its audience into a disturbed empathy
with him. No less provocative was the show's flirtation with
nihilism in consciously positioning itself – and its audience –
within the same symbiotic matrix of mass-media violence and
voyeurism it interrogated, by exploiting the trauma of lives
already shattered by Cunanan's actions in an entertainment
that was as lurid as it was politically sophisticated.

The book that did much of the heavy lifting the series
drew from is reporter Maureen Orth's extensive account of
Andrew Cunanan's life and killing spree, and the resultant
manhunt and media carnival. *Vulgar Favours* grew out of
a long-form piece for *Vanity Fair* – Cunanan's favourite
magazine – that Orth had already been commissioned to
write before the fugitive turned up in South Beach, Miami.
It was there, after lying low in sleazy hotels and gay bars,

that Cunanan murdered his fifth and most famous victim, before turning a gun on himself in a boathouse surrounded by TV-network helicopters and armed police.

Though written only two decades ago, the book promulgates certain prejudices that now seem laughable. Cunanan enjoyed drugs and pornography: 'Experts on serial-killer behaviour say the combination can be explosive.' The TV series' brazen nods to the film adaptation of Bret Easton Ellis's novel *American Psycho* turn out to be more than a brinkmanship of tastelessness: Cunanan was transfixed by Ellis's fiction, identifying heavily with his blank, dissipated rich kids. At a gay nightclub hours before he shot Versace in the head, someone asked Cunanan what he did for a living. 'I'm a serial killer,' came his blithe, Batemanesque reply.

Isn't it about time you grew out of such solipsistic ramblings? Is taking vast quantities of dangerous drugs something to celebrate? Especially since listening to someone's experiences on drugs is as tedious as listening to someone's dreams. And more importantly, do I care? The answer is simple. No. I'm not interested in your self-indulgent descriptions of your travels, your sexual fantasies, your masturbation. Especially when your sexual fantasies are distasteful to say the least, and usually misogynistic, often about young girls. The extended, graphic fantasy about a teenage student, whom you were teaching at the time, is particularly repugnant. And there are such banalities here too, expressed as though they are the revelation of profound truths. As a human being, you are insufferable – you are not good to women and remarkably solipsistic. You seem to think it's edgy to write down every sexist thought that crosses your mind, but in a world where sexist behaviour from straight men is the exhausting norm, this is not a daring narrative act – it just reads like more tedious everyday misogyny. Your characters are flimsy and one-dimensional. You come off as though you think you are the first person to have a high or a comedown. My problem with your work is the sheer amount of anti-homeless behaviour. There's homophobia sprinkled throughout too, because of course there is. Hurting people who are already disadvantaged isn't edgy. It's pathetic. All this self-indulgent navel-gazing: you are a man and yours is a life that just doesn't interest me. You tried way too hard to be cool. Like a teenage boy enveloped in a cloud of body spray, less would have been better. I found your desperate desire to be edgy cringeworthy. Your endings are pathetic, such stupid ways of wrapping it up. I'd stopped caring what happened about halfway through and it was a chore to get to the end. Utterly disappointing. Your novel is vile. I struggle even to form words through my seething hatred. Racist and toxic, misogynistic and violent, an unfortunate blot on the literary scene. Maybe society does keep you from acting on your violent urges, and granted, men still lust after all those 'untouchable' women and objectify them. I guess it makes sense why so many of your relationships are wrecked ships behind you. I regret buying this. It's without doubt one of the worst books I've read in quite some time, to the point where I'm actually angry at myself for wasting my time reading it. You certainly struggle with your baser urges. I cringe while reading such encounters: with this kind of writing, women don't have to imagine what men are thinking when they leer at them. Your privileged-seeming life experiences, your excessive self-involvement – it's annoying. Cheap shock tactics, depressing and pointless – absolute garbage. You think there's something edgy about this stuff you describe. As if it doesn't happen literally all of the time. As if there's a woman out there who hasn't had a guy make her uncomfortable at a party, or throw a temper tantrum because he felt his masculinity was hurt. It's boring and I'm over this being seen as exciting. It's all too tastelessly repulsive to maintain interest. Nothing goes on. It's just this sad festival of drugs all day long, all night long. Meaningless experiences that only leave you emptier. The crowd you're in with are just a bunch of sleazy, lazy people with first-world problems, who have never actually worked hard in their lives and think they're contributing to society by getting high and writing about nothing. Some might be tempted to call your style uncompromising, but I just find it a mix of pretentious and irritating. You enforce this idea that part of being an edgy nihilist is being abusive and an addict. The writing seems like it's trying hard to be shocking just for the sake of it – something it fails at being regardless. As you are now on the threshold of middle age, I suggest that you grow up and face the real world and leave your adolescent angst behind. I'd be ashamed to put my name to this thing. I give your book my first one star.

38 MARTIN AMIS

London Fields (1989)

For a couple of decades, resenting Martin Amis has been a British national pastime. Even his many admirers would struggle to deny that Amis goes looking for it: there's that hard kernel of invidiousness; that flair for the cruel putdown; that insistence on letting you know he reckons he's better than you (with 'you' being everyone who isn't Martin Amis, or at least Saul Bellow or Vladimir Nabokov).

What makes this effrontery so galling, of course, is that Amis almost certainly *is* better than you – if writing potent, dazzling sentences in the English language is something you measure yourself by. I recently watched the ill-starred film adaptation of Amis's career-high novel *London Fields* – it's nowhere near as bad as the cackling reviews and historically paltry box-office takings suggest. The film's wildlife-documentary focus on flayed male egos and gasping sexual want was a reminder of Amis's long-standing concern with just these questions of status, dominance, superiority and their dark corollary, humiliation. This being Martin Amis, it's specifically *male* humiliation we're talking about here. *London Fields* failed to make the 1989 Booker Prize shortlist, cock-blocked by two feminist judges who disapproved of its depiction of women. Even if you feel they had a point, can we nonetheless agree that in its architectonic splendour, visions of megacity entropy, and unremitting lingual charisma, *London Fields* stands damn near the summit of modern novelistic achievement?

In those sinister London Fields, men live under continuous threat of humiliation – through sex, money, status – and their primally frantic recourse lies in the humiliation of other men: letting them know you're better than them. It's pitch-dark in the solar glare of Amis's pre-apocalyptic London, but no novel has ever made me laugh so immoderately (Keith Talent!). It was hysterical laughter edged with fear: his women may be paper-thin objects of desire ('I *am* a male fantasy figure,' purrs death-dripping honeytrap Nicola Six), but his men are all in hell – a realm Amis knows too intimately to be beyond sympathy.

In Stoke Newington I shared a house with an English guy who was the manager of the parks of north-east London – a job that exposed him to the city's sinister underside, traversed by networks of tribe and crime – and a girl from Luxembourg who worked in publishing. She spent all her time in her room downstairs, the vines in the back garden creeping over her window to shut out the sunlight. One Friday in summertime, the parks manager and I stayed up till near dawn in the living room, getting high and drinking wine. I awoke late and groggy the following morning. As I was shakily fixing a coffee he came in the front door, looking rattled. We sat out in the back garden and at first he said nothing. Finally he told me he'd been called out after an hour's sleep to London Fields, where as we were inhaling lines and listening to grime a young woman had been gang-raped and viciously mutilated. I lived in that house for a couple of years – a happy time, relatively speaking. My short stories finally started getting published after I'd amassed many rejection notes. That was just as well, because I was approaching thirty and needed some sign that my goal of becoming a writer was no delusion. There were fitful nights consumed by this fear, 4 a.m. fever-visions of shame and failure. Each time a story was accepted or a publisher showed interest in the novel I was writing, the news would trigger an outsized and ungrounded euphoria. My ego was scrawny. I was nothing in the world, without status and low on inner resources. Minor triumphs could inflate me, and defeats leave me gutted. I had no idea what I would do with my life were I not to find recognition as a writer. The fascistic strain in my psyche, wont to meet anxiety not with compassion but harsh exhortation, articulated a brutal mantra: 'If you fail, you deserve to fail.' I knew that if I were to fail – if no publisher took on the book that all my friends knew I was writing – the words would taunt me to the grave, the sneer of a torturer who finally had me where he wanted me. The fear generated tremendous energy, and although I drank, drugged and sniffed after all the sex I could get, my discipline was not wanting. There was another maxim I adopted in those days, comical where the first was cruel: Woody Allen's observation that 'Eighty per cent of success is showing up'. Hearing that quip really was encouraging. You just had to go at it hard, persist where others trailed off, not because they lacked talent but because they couldn't be bothered. If you wanted it enough, it would happen – by default. My small bedroom looked onto a back garden where at night I would sometimes hear foxes copulating, an eerie noise like infants in distress. The room filled up with printouts of novels, stories, lyrics. My Vietnamese girlfriend was living in the States and would come to stay for the three-month periods that her tourist visa allowed. I was in deep, thrown out of equilibrium by her depth of feeling and sensualism, her grace and integrity, her sense of style and her almost supernatural beauty. I wanted to own her completely, gorge on her while giving her such pleasure and excitement in return that she was bonded to me forever. The idea of her being with anyone else was unbearable. Her traditionalism from another time; a chastity that was mine alone to defile – I took these as marks of her fineness and rarity in a degraded era. Despite implying (through lies of omission) that I'd be as monogamous as I wanted her to be, after an initial lapse or two during our long stretches apart I hardly even tried to be faithful. London was a pheromone storm of temptation, and there was little I couldn't justify to myself in those days, especially at 3 a.m. in some warehouse rave with a headful of wine and chemicals. If the misandrist reader is wishing me retribution for my hypocrisy and white-boy entitlement, they can rest easy knowing that when it came, it came prolonged and woeful. But that was later, and yes, those were happy days in north London – the happiness of someone who sights a goal whose attainment will redeem his squalid life, but who suspects he is happier now than he ever will be after that attainment. I wrote and sent out my work. I made music. I watched my girl perform stripteases on video-chat from across the Atlantic. We roamed the city together when she was over for a summer, then I wouldn't see her for months. I got on okay with the people I lived with. Our reclusive flatmate intrigued me, down there in her vine-shaded bedroom, but I never learned much about her. Once her younger sister came to visit. I was in a band at the time, playing seedy and sincere electropop. The two sisters came to watch us perform at a venue in Hackney. I remember looking down from the stage and being struck by the younger sister's haunted face, her distant eyes. Some months later she was to commit suicide, a young woman at what would have been the outset of her life. Afterwards I moved to San Francisco, began a new phase, and lost touch with both my former flatmates.

39 JOAN DIDION

Play It As It Lays (1970)

Lo and behold, the sixties seem interesting again. As we witness the implosion of the American empire – with orgasmic *Schadenfreude* or appalled concern, depending on how black and bitter and sick of this worldwide American life our hearts have grown – that prior period of vast cultural mutation appears as a warped lysergic montage rolling to a Lana Del Rey soundtrack, in which we squintingly perceive some message about what is unfurling now. Joan Didion's celebrated essay collections, *Slouching Towards Bethlehem* and *The White Album*, chronicled the era from the jangled viewpoint of a conservative woman repelled and fascinated by the dark Dionysian energies unleashed by an orgiastic new culture.

In those essays, as in Didion's superb novel of LA desolation *Play It As It Lays*, motive and causality have disappeared from human affairs: terror and chaos unfold in a void as pristine and meaningless as the Californian desert. Set among the vampires and spectres of the movie business, *Play It As It Lays* isn't really a plot novel. Maria, a thirty-one-year-old actress in career decline, has an abortion, divorces her film-director husband and begins to psychically disintegrate. Atmosphere is everything – the cool, slant, mysterious prose style has aged well. The swimming pools and beach houses of Didion's California define a zone of nihilistic dread – 'the dead still centre of the world, the quintessential intersection of nothing' – where men are cold and violent, women glazed and anaesthetised. Maria drives aimlessly along the freeways, firing a pistol at road signs. At her nadir she winds up in Las Vegas, where she wanders for several lost weeks.

The tone of muffled panic and bleak sedation is gradually submerged by images of horror: a nuclear test bomb detonates beneath the desert; children burn to death in a locked car, 'the little faces, helpless screams'. In this glaring American vacuum explanations are scarce and hollow figures gesture without significance: 'She sat on the rattan chaise in the hot October twilight and watched BZ throw the ice cubes from his drink one by one into the swimming pool.'

One Friday night while drinking alone in a bar in downtown San Francisco, I fell talking to a tough, heavyset man in late middle age who was putting away jars of high-content IPA. He was surly, irascible, but after a while he seemed to lay down his defences. Let's say his name was Bill O'Rourke. He had served in Vietnam. His experiences during the war led him afterwards to study the biological basis of life. It was a fact beyond morality, he said, that life forms exert themselves with the utmost vigour to annihilate entities they deem to be a threat – and that's what war is, there's no sense feeling remorse for killing done in combat. He had served as a pilot, flying bombing raids over Vietnam and Cambodia. On one mission he flew low over the jungle, approaching his target, an enemy-occupied village that he suddenly realised was far more heavily defended than had been anticipated. Other pilots began to break formation and abort. He knew his life was in extreme peril, but he had made a commitment. He said to himself, 'My name is Bill O'Rourke, my word is my bond,' and locked his sights on the target. His plane streaked over the village, somehow avoiding flak, and delivered its payload, incinerating the enemy in a napalm flash. He told the story with defiant pride, daring me to voice a liberal beta cuck's reproach. A short while later I mentioned that the woman I was living with was Vietnamese, and that she had moved with her family to America as a little girl after her father, a lieutenant in the South Vietnamese army, was released from the concentration camp where he'd been held

175

captive for years. He thought about this a moment, then slowly nodded his head. We drank a few more IPAs, and when he started getting surly again and jabbing a finger in my chest, I thought I'd best call it a night.

40 DAVID MARKSON

Reader's Block (1996)

There are significant novelists whose work is propelled by a confidence in the novel form's inexhaustibility, the belief that it can do anything. Then there are those whose achievement emerges from a struggle against a sense of depletion or weariness, of no longer being enlivened by the conventional strategies of prose fiction. Such novelists sometimes produce their most vital work right at the point when they're ready to give up on the novel entirely.

David Markson was almost seventy when *Reader's Block*, the first in his extraordinary series of late novels, was published. In these books, Markson succeeded at that most attractive ambition held by those seeking new pathways for the novel: he removed almost all the traditional furniture of setting, plot and character development, and delivered a captivating read nonetheless.

The protagonist of *Reader's Block* is 'Reader' (in *This Is Not a Novel* it will be 'Writer'; in *Vanishing Point*, 'Author', and in *The Last Novel*, 'Novelist'). Reader is alone, melancholy and old. His mind is cluttered with desultory impressions from a lifetime among books. And here comes Markson's stroke of genius: the flesh of his late novels is composed of bite-size anecdotes and quotations from the lives and works of writers and artists, and these, through repetition and patterning, cohere into themes – and a sort of narrative.

Fragments such as 'Robert Walser spent his last twenty-seven years in a mental institution' are entwined with Reader's ruminations on the barrenness of his winter years and the transience of all things. The literary flotsam and jetsam mirrors his late-life concerns: decay, regret, solitude, the meaning of a life devoted to literature. Like other Markson protagonists, he dwells on suicide, madness, alcoholism and despair – art's immemorial companions, Markson will have us remember. And death too – death is all over these books.

David Markson's four anti-novels are as addictive as smack – and they're all quite alike, as Markson admitted. But then, he noted, no one ever hassled Monet for painting so many water lilies in his mature years, now did they?

When I was in my late twenties I went through a phase of reading a lot of male novelists in their sixties. I think I wanted to get a sense of the terrain ahead, imagining that that would help me (the likelier truth is that no matter how well you think you know the terrain up front, when you get there it's always a bewildering tundra). That was the period when I read David Markson, or rather when I read his later works – everything after Wittgenstein's Mistress. *It was winter and I had moved temporarily to Boston, to be with my girlfriend who was studying for an MFA in poetry there. A few days before Christmas we took a Greyhound bus to New York. On the journey I read one of Markson's books and then, when we got to New York, I immediately went out to buy the rest of them from the Strand bookstore. Reading novels was a distraction from the bitter fallings-out my girlfriend and I used to have; not speaking for days and sometimes weeks on end, both too stubborn to be the first to yield. (I told a friend about these rows and he concluded that I had little hope of defeating a Vietnamese woman in a contest of wills: had her indomitable race not brought the American empire to its knees?) We had one such row on Christmas Eve, storming away from each other in Central Park under a bright winter sky as carol singers entertained cheery families. We were staying in a hotel off Times Square. On Christmas Day it began to snow, and soon New York was snowed under. All the roads in and out were closed. After some pleading, the hotel manager agreed to let us stay on at a lower rate till we were able to leave town. It should have been romantic, but beyond the angry silence, what I mostly remember is drinking nerve-wasting coffee from a machine in the hotel lobby, watching the snow trucks clearing the street, and wondering if the worst was behind me or loomed up ahead.*

41 HERMAN MELVILLE

Moby-Dick; or, The Whale (1851)

Borges suggested that all great literature eventually becomes children's literature: in time, even sprawling narratives assume the compact shape of bedtime stories. *Moby-Dick*, a novel as hefty as its titular whale and roomy as the sea he swims in, could, with severe Gordon Lish-style editing, be pared down to novella or even – since we're being sacrilegious – short-story length, if narrative were the true quarry. Some 500 pages in, its author-narrator Ishmael undergoes an attack of vertigo on realising that the tale of obsession he is telling – that of Captain Ahab's hell-bent quest for vengeance on the whale who tore off his leg – has itself become a pullulating, all-devouring monstrosity of obsession, with its 'outreaching comprehensiveness of sweep, as if to include the whole circle of the sciences, and all the generations of whales, and men, and mastodons, past, present, and to come, with all the revolving panoramas of empire on earth and throughout the universe, not excluding its suburbs'. In this mad moment of revelation (everything about the book is gloriously mad), form mirrors content as *Moby-Dick* becomes the insatiable Leviathan that will not cease till it has exhausted itself and its reader in a maniacal bid to categorise all things on heaven and earth; or, at least, all you might ever want to know, and much you would not, concerning cetology, whaling, seafaring and even – a nine-page chapter on this – the boundless metaphysical horror supposedly evoked by white, the colour of the dread whale.

The language is all-American apocalyptic high style, like Cormac McCarthy channelling Shakespeare at his most hysterical ('I'm demoniac, I am madness maddened!'), and it's surprisingly funny too. Herman Melville probably ought to have blown his brains out after this one, his work down here well done. Both in its epic story of monomaniacal pursuit, and the extravagant nature of its telling, *Moby-Dick* bears witness to mankind's – and the most ambitious authors' – propensity, if we can be Nietzschean about it, to wreck themselves against infinity.

There's a question hanging over this whole endeavour that I can't put off voicing any longer: what kind of writer spends his time composing a book from other people's books? More simply put, have I nothing better to do? Of course, I'm being somewhat facetious here. I like works that take existing materials and construct from them something new – in this case, a composite autoportrait in readings that has further become, quite unexpectedly, a report on how the end of the world as we know it is looking from my particular balcony. Nevertheless, I feel like answering the question: what kind of writer am I? If I were to snap a prosaic selfie, a pointillist screen-grab of who I am now so that I might slip out of him and into someone more comfortable, I might begin by saying that I am thirty-seven years old. That I have no children, and it's probable I will never have any. That I've made one woman pregnant, that I know about. That when people tell me about their children, I don't make enough of an effort to seem interested, and they stop. That I haven't read Anna Karenina *(though I would like to) or the novels of Jane Austen. That I've begun to regret not having had a happier life. That I've been to five therapists, the first for three years; the second for a few months; the third on and off for about a year; the fourth for a few weeks (in Berlin); and the fifth for a couple of months. That I feel I'd benefit from seeing a female therapist, but it hasn't happened yet. That my attitudes are often reactions to what I perceive as other people's moral self-flattery. That I was shouted at while stepping into a mosque. That I don't recall being inside a synagogue, though*

*I did take part in a ritual Jewish feast. That I suffer more from
ageing than other people I know, because I fetishise youth more.
That I'm encouraged to find that sexual desire evolves as you
get older, becomes more versatile and diffuse. That after falling
in love with an Asian woman and then losing her, I worried
that Western women would thereafter seem coarse and cor-
rupted. That I feel as though I've failed important tests. That
I have little interest in telling stories – or reading them – as an
end in itself. That I prefer the journals, the essays, the periph-
eral writings, to the novels and short stories. That I suspect
when you've lived a certain amount of time, it's impossible to
entirely like yourself. That if, when it came to the end of my
life, I was offered the chance to live it over again, exactly as
it had been, I think I wouldn't take it, though I don't believe
this means my life won't have been worthwhile. That I've been
in an earthquake – in Bogotá. That I've never been inside a
slaughterhouse. That I've had panic attacks in various cities.
That I once lived on the tenth floor. That I remember my first
orgasm. That I don't know the name of the first girl I went to
bed with, nor how many women I've slept with. That I've never
made love with a man, and though I've sometimes imagined
what that would be like, I don't feel I've missed out by not
having had the experience. That I prefer the villain. That
I have regrets, but only in an abstract sense, in that it seems
to me life unfolds as it unfolds, we're not in control of it the
way we imagine ourselves to be. That there are things I never
got over. That I believe the compulsion to write is intimately
linked to a wound. That I'm receptive to the possibility of some
form of continued existence after death, while accepting that
death might mean total extinction. That if I were to name the*

'writer of my life', the way I once read César Aira doing (with reference to Lautréamont), it would probably be Friedrich Nietzsche, though I know he won't speak to the second half of my life the way he did to the first. That I've never told someone I loved them without meaning it. That I fear obsolescence. That I fear humiliation. That I was on Facebook for several years, and after deleting my account never regretted doing so. That I've been on Twitter for almost a decade, with long periods of dormancy, and although I dislike it, I feel it would be imprudent to delete my account. That I've been on Instagram for a year. That I've never used LinkedIn or TikTok. That I have used Myspace and LiveJournal. That I have used Tinder and Bumble. That I remember cassettes, videos, CDs, LimeWire. That I'm moved when I think of Albert Camus's definition of manliness: never humiliating anyone. That I've voted five times: twice in referendums, twice in Irish elections, and once in a UK election. That I've sometimes thought I can feel a purer love for a man than I can for a woman, because it isn't complicated by sex. That I was bullied as a child for being weird, for having big ears. That several women told me I have a beautiful penis. That I used to tell myself I ought to read more poetry, but over the years the admonishment quietened. That I'm drawn to empty beaches and often they find their way into my books. That when I was a kid I wrote a letter to a Manchester United football player, and received a standard-issue card from the club in response, thanking me for my support. That I collected Panini stickers. That I played marbles in the schoolyard. That I was good at maths, at everything, till I got into drinking and bands. That I've made enemies. That in India a middle-aged Israeli woman told me that from the moment she saw my face, she knew I was filled with longing. That I'm ashamed. That I have no idea what my future holds, who will be around when I die. That I haven't built much of a future. That I'm creatively happy. That I consider the arguments in favour of vegetarianism to be persuasive, though I continue to eat meat. That I've always been afraid of fish. That eels evoke in me a deeper emotion than fear, a primal horror. That I don't believe I'm on the right side of history. That I don't want to die, but if it were to happen I wouldn't want it to be considered tragic. That I cried easily as a child, and when I cried in front of my father I felt humiliated and enraged. That I never wrote a book without salt and vinegar Pringles appearing in it. That I knew a girl in Colombia who left on her red silk scarf while we made love – and that I'd forgotten this detail until I read it in an old journal I found in a drawer. That in the same journal, I read about a sexual encounter I had at a writing retreat which I'd forgotten all about. That my early sexual experiences were humiliating, and I've never fully separated sex from humilia-tion. That my feelings towards liberated sex are complicated because I perceive sex to be indissociable from hierarchy and exclusion. That I hold women to a different set of standards to men. That there are people I haven't forgiven. That the worse it gets, the better I feel. That in the mornings I like coffee from my moka pot, and smoothies made with bananas and oat milk. That I believe I've inflicted irreparable harm. That I remember the sound of a passing train while lying in bed on a childhood holiday. That I believe art can be a kind of redemption. That I've always had good teeth.

Stalingrad (1998)

Of the many places one would not wish to be in the twentieth century, few are less appealing than the city of Stalingrad and its surroundings between August 1942 and February 1943. The awesome scale of the carnage described in Antony Beevor's magisterial, celebrated tome of military history suggests that, irrespective of the warring ideological systems for which hundreds of thousands of soldiers and civilians died, and the colossal folly of the whole endeavour, merely being there was enough to constitute heroism.

When Hitler launched his attack on the Soviet Union with Operation Barbarossa, he intended to annihilate Bolshevism itself – or, more accurately, its sinister mutation, Stalinism. When his armies finally reached Stalingrad on the banks of the Volga, more was at stake than the symbolism carried by the city's name: among historians it is widely accepted that the ensuing catastrophe for the German forces marked the turning point in the Second World War, and thus the high-water mark of the Third Reich.

And what a catastrophe it was. If you're the kind of reader who is spurred on by phrases like 'savage fighting' and 'battle of annihilation' appearing every few pages, *Stalingrad* will keep you lit. We all know the story of the largest confrontation in the history of warfare, more or less: the staggering numbers of Soviet soldiers executed by their own side for 'cowardice' and 'treason'; the hell-on-earth intensity of the aerial bombardment and house-by-house street fighting; the final encirclement and devastation of the German Sixth Army, laid low like others before them by the severity of the Russian winter. Beevor's achievement is in taking these big, head-spinning historical facts and animating them with pace and eye-catching detail, making a *read* of it all.

After the defeat at Stalingrad, Hitler was a diminished man, as vengeful Soviet armies marched west towards Berlin. Like the Armageddon it depicts, *Stalingrad* also represents a turning point: following its success, military history burst out of its niche to become a bestselling genre.

*Today I'm bored. I haven't been bored in quite some time,
and not since the lockdown began. We seem to be moving
out of the novelty phase of this global rupture, into the phase
of tedium, of realising that the end might recede perpetually.
Everything is cancelled, everyone is uncertain. Me, I've got
what I've always wanted – for something to happen, although
even before this, things were happening at a helter-skelter
rate. Boredom had come to seem a nineties phenomenon, like
grunge or Britpop. But now something so big has happened
that it's stopped anything else from being able to happen.
I'm tempted to go stand in a socially distanced queue outside the supermarket and buy some wine, break my rule of
drinking only at weekends. The other day I took a Valium
and lay on the beach, dozed off with the sound of the surf
in my ears. I'd been staring so long at screens that when
I opened my eyes and saw a seabird glide past it seemed
as finely pixellated as anything else. We're all having our
sombre realisations at the same time. A borderline friend
texted this morning, saying her life is acutely painful now,
she doesn't feel much motivation to go on, that 'there's no
life left'. At the weekend I video-chatted with a friend in
Dublin. He was alone in his flat, sniffing cocaine and drinking.
He mentioned his mother and then told me, with mirth-
ful sincerity, that it would have been better if she'd never
given birth to him – better for her, for him, for the world.
His admission provoked a fit of hysterical laughter such as
I haven't experienced in years – uncontrollable laughter that*

made tears pour down my cheeks and my stomach cramp, X-ray flashes of distress amidst the hilarity. Another friend is stuck at home with a woman – his wife of many years – from whom he had agreed to separate just before the quarantine began. He says it's torture. Alcoholics are relapsing, addicts are in forced withdrawal. The depressed sink further into a dejection mirrored in a planet whose horizons have shrunk. Economists talk on podcasts of another Great Depression, the possibility of 'systemic collapse'. True, the culture's bullshit is being swept away, for a while at least, exposed as stupid and fraudulent – but everything else is swept away too, and the victory is hollow. Celebrities post videos in unflattering light, from their beds or their bathtubs, with panic in their eyes, as if they expect to be slung up on hooks when civic order crumbles. The Queen of England appears on television to tell her subjects, 'We'll meet again.' The most famous man on earth suggests we inject bleach and heal ourselves with light – one of those astounding, generation-defining moments that seem now to happen every month or so. The friend who texted of her despair tells me: it's as if the wind changed and we all got frozen as we were before this happened, and now we're stuck with ourselves. Meanwhile, I'm running out of books. In a pile in a drawer I found one I hadn't read: the journal kept by a photographer named Alix Cléo Roubaud in the years before her death at the age of thirty-one. She endured depression, self-hatred and anxiety, which she medicated with alcohol and sleeping pills. She died not by suicide, but of a bodily ailment. The final entry, dated 19 January 1983 and eccentrically punctuated, reads:

*It took a fatal illness, or one recorded as such, to cure
me of wanting to die. In the most oblique, organic, slow
manner, I, in a way, invented my own illness.*

—and the one from which I will never recover.

43 VIRGINIE DESPENTES

Baise-Moi (1994)

Translated by Bruce Benderson

Virginie Despentes must have written her first novel with a wrap of speed, a bottle of whiskey and an overflowing ashtray cluttering the desk. If you're looking for rounded characters and subtle insights into the human heart, best head for the exit right now. *Baise-Moi* is a fast, ludicrous, superficial kill-streak of a novel that fuses the extremist strain in French fiction – Sade, Bataille, Genet – with pulp aesthetics and road-movie romanticism.

The plot? Two young women, sick and tired of society, men, the middle class and everything else, load up on guns and embark on a murderous rampage across France, fuelled by liquor, sex and weed. That's it. Despentes would go on to direct a notorious film adaptation whose porn-star cast, un-simulated sex and extreme violence would see it banned in France and beyond.

French culture can seem like a museum of itself, where the aura of refinement and reverence for the past are stifling. Despentes's liveliness owes much to her schooling in punk, with its snarling disdain for respectable taste and bourgeois convention. *Baise-Moi* is a novel by a writer bored with novels, more turned on by *Grand Theft Auto*, slasher movies and porn. Despentes has since mellowed out, to a degree. Her most affecting writing is in *King Kong Theory*, where she recounts her time spent working as a prostitute in prose that wavers between shame and defiance, empathy and disgust.

Baise-Moi is all cheap thrills and homicidal delirium. You can tell Despentes got her kicks while knocking it out. It's a nihilist fantasy delivering what many of us have longed to do at some point or another: step into a crowd and blast anything that moves. Despentes can't have known that scenarios like that of *Baise-Moi* would play out for real on the streets of twenty-first century France – the rage of the *banlieues* spewing death and mayhem over comfortable society, all those avenging angels striding through gun smoke, exalted with hate, merciless and ready to die.

The first time I moved to Paris I lived there for the best part of a year, then I returned to Ireland to pass a solitary winter on the Wexford coast. The Friday night after I left Paris, I began watching The Hunger Games on TV. My laptop was open beside me and it seemed from glancing at Twitter that something was kicking off in France. I tried to watch the film and not succumb to distraction, but soon it was impossible: scenes of war were unfolding in the streets where I'd strolled and hung out just days earlier. A year later I was living in the city again. The first anniversary of the November attacks fell on a gloomy day, a dense grey such as you only get in Paris, the sun buried deep in the overcast. Parisians placed flowers outside the Carillon bar, the Petit Cambodge, the Bataclan. A man whose son had been murdered came on the radio, saying he refused to take part in the official ceremony because to do so would be to dishonour his pain, give the false impression that he had somehow processed his grief, contemplated forgiveness. We watched a flotilla of paper lanterns being sent out on the Canal Saint Martin, and for a while Paris seemed like Varanasi, where each evening at sunset the Hindus light thousands of candles and set them to float down the Ganges, an offering to the god in the river.

44 MAX FRISCH

From the Berlin Journal (1973–4)

Translated by Wieland Hoban

Even before life became a primarily online phenomenon, some literary commentators were noticing a shift in interest away from the novel towards textual forms traditionally considered supplementary: journals, diaries, notebooks, correspondence. This trend has only accelerated as we become habituated to observing one another's lives in unprecedented detail. The immediacy of the connected world stokes an impatience with fictive artifice; we are disinclined to read about invented people when the real ones around us are so very interesting. More cynically, it might be said that the culture of oversharing, aestheticised selfhood and personal branding has infiltrated literary production – writers have never been more fascinated by themselves. Whatever the cause, there is a distinct drift away from fiction, as the novel mutates towards forms bearing resemblances to the journal, memoir and autobiography.

Max Frisch is among the most respected of Swiss novelists, and he may be one of the best too, but I wouldn't know because I've only read his journals and sketchbooks. Anticipating our twenty-first century reality hunger, Frisch regarded the journal (qua diary written for a public audience) as a literary form, and when he moved to Berlin in the 1970s at the age of sixty-one, he began one that he intended eventually to stand among his *oeuvre* (because of the sensitive nature of some of the entries, he put a twenty-year retention period after his death on the Berlin journal's publication).

There seems to be something in the practice of journal-keeping that encourages a gloomy tone, as if turning the gaze inwards to dwell on one's thought processes stifles levity and amplifies morbidity. From the outset, Frisch is preoccupied with death and ageing: 'The awareness that I have three or four years, decent years, left.' Booze is another worry – 'The battle against alcohol, no week without a defeat on that front'. Above all, Frisch is obsessed by intimations of creative and cognitive decline; *From the Berlin Journal* is a claustrophobic document of a brain grinding itself down observing its own progressive entropy, real or imagined.

Usually, keeping a diary is the kind of project I begin with a firm resolve that quickly sags – but not always. When I was younger, the assumption behind diary-keeping was that a particular period in my life, being rich with incident, or playing out someplace that bestowed an automatic interest on even the quotidian, might serve later as the basis for a novel. Occasionally though, I've kept diaries not as the raw material for a future work, but to transcribe the present in a real-time text that was intended as the work itself. When I spent a couple of years drifting around Asia and South America, I kept one such journal, shared daily on a blogging site. A decade later, while living in Berlin I scrupulously kept another journal over a four-month period. Each morning I typed in bed to distil the events of the day before, alongside musings on literature and writing. I inserted quotations from books I was reading, described the city's streets and cafés and train lines, and documented my then complicated love life. I initially titled the file 'Berlin Diary', then changed it to 'Autumn Diary', and finally to 'Valium Diary' (it contained many such entries as: 'I take half a Diazepam. Midnight.'). I ceased writing it on New Year's Day, by which time the text amounted to some fifty thousand words. I later pared it down to five thousand. A couple of years on, the journal reads uncomfortably, a document of loneliness and torment. In one passage, I noted that to the mind racked by anxiety and regret, every room you dwell in is a prison cell. Here and now, in the cheer of spring on the Wexford coast, I affirm the inverse: that when a degree of inner relief is attained, you can enjoy a sense of liberation and expansiveness even as the world closes down. And yet, when I look across at him from here, that tortured and isolated man in a bare room in Berlin seems to me to have got what he'd always wanted. At the nadir of his loneliness, he was living his dream – which turned out, no surprise, to be a nightmare more dire than he could have imagined. I don't believe I could survive such bleakness again. I don't really believe I could survive it at the time either. Perhaps, in some quantum, many-worlds sense, he's still over there, as I'm here; we've split, diverged, and whereas I couldn't take it any more, choosing in desperation to save myself, he's still going at it hard, stripping existence right back to the bone, plunging in deeper till he gets close up to the essence. At which point I'll hear on the coastal breeze the phantom echo of a gunshot, or the snap of a tautening rope, or the rattle of pills as they scatter on the floor – the grand romance, brought to its dismal and cinematic climax, the one I never had the guts for. Or perhaps – and this is in some sense the darker thought – perhaps I've shirked my destiny right when I was on its threshold, evaded my true mission and deepest desire. A few weeks ago I began a course of antidepressant medication, something I had resisted my entire adult life. And the meds are working – working so well I wonder why I shook my head all those times when doctors or therapists urged me to consider a course of SSRIs. Here alone in my quarantine by the sea, I smile involuntarily. I am zestful, productive. My thoughts ring sharp and clear. I have a handle on my demons, see ways to confront and resolve my problems. Really, I've never felt better. And all I can think is that I've betrayed him.

45 LA ROCHEFOUCAULD

Moral Reflections or Sententiae and Maxims (1678)

Translated by E.H. Blackmore and A.M. Blackmore

Until not so long ago, cynicism was the thing. It wasn't just Generation X: much modern literature favoured a sceptical, mocking outlook that probed righteousness for ulterior motives. What we might call the Justin Trudeauification of networked life in the 2010s demoted cynicism in favour of showy goodness, but behind the shit-eating grin and nice-guy schtick, the same human animal remained. Banished by millennial Manichaeism from our bright public spaces, the Shadow gained power in the offline dark, till it came roaring back with an orange comb-over (if not in blackface).

We ought to go on a corporate retreat to help us Reconnect With Our Buried Cynicism, and I know what book to bring. In the 1600s, a French aristocrat in his forties peeled back the skin of societal appearances to reveal the squirming, unlovely truth beneath. La Rochefoucauld intended his collection of incisive observations to stand as a 'portrait of man's heart', admitting that it was 'full of truths unaccept-able to human pride'. Across 504 aphorisms, he exposes apparent virtue as vice or weakness in disguise. Self-flattery is led out naked and shivering for pitiless scrutiny. Not lost on La Rochefoucauld is how we tend to grow more 'virtu-ous' in tandem with our declining capacity to do wrong:

'When vices leave us, we flatter ourselves that we are the ones leaving them.'

The aphorist Don Paterson has noted – in an aphorism – that aphorisms 'all sound as if they were delivered by the same disenfranchised, bad-tempered minor deity'. La Rochefoucauld set the tone. 'No one deserves to be praised for kindness if he does not have the strength to be bad,' he writes, and centuries later Nietzsche will accord: 'Verily, I have often laughed at the weaklings who thought themselves good because they had no claws.' An even closer match: La Rochefoucauld's 'What makes us unable to bear the vanity of other people is the fact that it wounds our own' mutates into Nietzsche's 'The vanity of others runs counter to our taste only when it runs counter to our vanity.'

RD: *Would you say much has changed in the four centuries since you penned your maxims? Would you update anything?*

LR: *The truths I illuminated concerning the nature of man are immutable and not delimited by history. Man's moral nature does not evolve, though its outer disguises and subterfuges may. As you so cleverly demonstrated by comparing my words to those of the German philologist, subsequent efforts have been iterations of my findings. My descendants have simply added ornamentation.*

RD: *And of those aphorists and* moralistes *who followed you, whom do you rate?*

LR: *The obvious ones. My judgements in this matter are not heterodox.*

RD: *You've perhaps noticed that the celebrated aphorists all share the quality of being male. Do you think we've seen evidence more recently of the emergence of a specifically female aphoristic style, capable of mining insights that are perhaps inaccessible to male experience?*

LR: *I might point out that my own efforts were spurred on by my participation in the salon established by Madeleine de Souvré, the marquise de Sablé, who engaged in her own* moralisme *and achieved some pithy formulations. There was a band of us at it, you see. We would work privately and then convene to share our productions, discussing them together. An excellent stimulus. It's true that the marquise deemed mine to be the more valuable coinages, and I shan't* dispute her. As for the question of a distinctly feminine aphoristic style, I have indeed observed the emergence of a smattering of lady moralistes in recent years, though their efforts so far have been, I regret to say, generally inferior.

RD: You wouldn't recommend even one?

LR: Females in general would do better not to write, I daresay. It is an activity ill-suited to their temperament; it uglifies them. The esteemed marquise, of course, being an exception.

RD: You can't say that.

LR: I'm from the seventeenth century, my boy. We do things differently here.

RD: I see. Do you ever regret so ruthlessly exposing human self-interest and hypocrisy? I mean, do you feel it helped open the floodgates to an epoch of cynicism, an erosion of decency, an undermining of the illusions human beings need to maintain about themselves to avoid a fatal demoralisation, as it were?

LR: Undoubtedly my efforts quickened and in some sense perhaps even instigated these world-historic processes you adumbrate. However, ideas appear on the horizon at their appointed hour, and then there can be no suppressing them. I served as a vessel. Had I been thwarted, someone elsewhere would have reached identical conclusions before too long, and you would perhaps be questioning him now instead of me. Darwin, Freud, Marx, modern science – all of that was still to come. Unquestionably, man was in for a rough few centuries in terms of his self-image. One can only be told so often that one is nothing but an animal before one starts to behave accordingly.

RD: Do you regard yourself as a misanthrope?

LR: *I regard myself as a courtier, a military man, and a bon vivant. The fact that I don't trust my fellow man as far as I can throw him diminishes not one jot the pleasure I take in life. And now, if you don't mind, it is the hour of the aperitif. After we dine, quarantined here at the chalet, the marquise and I intend to binge some content. Life is rich, my boy. Seize it while the blood runs hot in your veins!*

Memories, Dreams, Reflections (1961)

Translated by Clara Winston and Richard Winston

When I was a student of psychoanalysis at Trinity College, Carl Jung was a figure of faint derision. We were expected to read Sigmund Freud, Melanie Klein and Jacques Lacan, whereas Jung was for your woolly-brained aunt who attends crystal-healing workshops. Beginning to suspect that the bleak materialism into which I had been educated was an inadequate framework of understanding – and that fashion and tribalism are as rife among intellectuals as they are anywhere else – I took an extracurricular interest in Jung's work, and found it triggered plenty of the paradigm-rocking insights that came thick and fast during that period of life.

To be accurate, I didn't read Jung so much as the Jungians – the writers who took on the task of communicating Jung's often stodgily expressed ideas in more inviting prose. The one primary text that did leave a major impression on me was not straightforwardly written by Jung either. When he was in his eighties, Jung had a series of recorded conversations with his colleague and secretary Aniela Jaffé, and the pair shaped from these raw materials as richly strange an autobiography as I've read.

Jung acknowledges off the bat that he has little interest in retreading the 'outer' events of his life: you won't find much on who he slept with, nor on his friendships and enmities, bar the one with his great Oedipal frenemy Freud. For Jung, the purpose of life is to make conscious the unconscious self in order to achieve individuation. The royal roads to integrated selfhood are myth, symbol and storytelling, whereas rationalism and doctrinairism are 'the disease of our time; they pretend to have all the answers'. *Memories, Dreams, Reflections* is Jung's personal myth: 'Whether or not these stories are "true" is not the problem. The only question is whether what I tell is *my* fable, *my* myth.' The marvellous visions he goes on to describe suggest that, to borrow from Salvador Dalí, the only difference between Carl Jung and a madman is that Carl Jung was not a madman.

The writer Paul Preciado suggests that our most brilliant dreams deserve to be introduced into autobiography, as they are no less vivid or significant than events in our waking lives. Certain dreams give me the impression of being something like memories of the future, the rumble of great events, outer or inner, towards which we are drifting. Such dreams are the roar of the waterfalls that draw us downstream even when, in waking life, we believe ourselves to be floating on a calm and picturesque river. I include here a dream I wrote about for a magazine, a dream as indelible as any disaster or success I've encountered while awake:

> *The night she told me she loved me, I dreamed I was a passenger in an aeroplane that went down far out over the ocean. I swam from the wreckage and reached the shore of a tropical island. Clambering through the jungle, I came to a clearing where dozens of dancers were being directed in an elaborate choreography by a towering figure I knew to be Satan. Irresistibly, and in terror, I was compelled to join the dance, whose end point I understood to be my annihilation. On waking, I tried to tell myself that the nightmare was not prophecy; in the years that followed, after I moved to another continent to be with her, I kept trying.*

47 J.G. BALLARD

The Atrocity Exhibition (1970)

The J.G. Ballard book that should grace every home is not *Crash*, nor even *The Atrocity Exhibition*, but *Extreme Metaphors: Selected Interviews with J.G. Ballard 1967–2008*. In Ballard's interviews the ideas teem with intoxicating abundance, whereas the novels that serve as vehicles for those ideas tend to be clunky and long-winded, their plots and cut-out characters the paraphernalia of an entertainment form unsuited to the agitated twenty-first century brain that Ballard in other ways anticipated. Ballard was such a superb commentator on his own fiction, one wonders whether the fiction was needed at all. Might he not have simply pretended it existed, then given us books of pure ideation?

In the 1960s, Ballard wrote *The Atrocity Exhibition*, his most deliriously experimental novel, which wore its indebtedness to William Burroughs (whom Ballard revered 'to the other side of idolatry') on its sleeve. For a 1990 reissue, he annotated the novel with reflections and anecdotes. When I first read the book, I found the fiction as drastic and incoherent as a DMT trip, whereas the notes were highly stimulating. In them, Ballard freestyles on surrealist art and perverse sexuality, recounts such capers as putting on an exhibition of crashed cars, and affirms his literary indebtedness to the insane ('I owe them everything').

The Atrocity Exhibition obsesses over the ways in which violent mass-media spectacles – Vietnam, the assassination of JFK, the suicide of Marilyn Monroe – send shockwaves across the electric circuits of the global unconscious. Today it reads as an analogue to life on the internet: twenty tabs open on porn, war, ads, torture and celebrity razzmatazz.

Despite the cold brutality and psychotic carnage, there is no gloom here. Ballard was at heart a surrealist comedian and a perverse optimist: he wanted us to immerse ourselves in the destructive element, give free rein to the boundless psychopathology provoked by media technology. Let's watch the GoPro slaughters, jihadi snuff films and amputee porn, he might have said – and then we'll see what the robust and indomitable human race mutates into.

As I write this, I'm waiting to watch myself being interviewed in what I assume is among the planet's first ever digital literary festivals. It was originally supposed to take place, in the antediluvian sense of living bodies gathered and proximate, on the west coast of Ireland. Instead it's happening in the homes of the writers, hosts and audiences. Due to technical concerns, rather than film my event live, the festival organisers recorded it earlier this morning and will broadcast it shortly – in three minutes – with the audience having no reason not to assume it's live. The upshot of this temporal disjunction is that I can sit back in the atomised crowd and observe myself, as if I'm his evil twin. Maybe I'll heckle him. Or maybe I'll develop a weird crush, approach him after the festival with fervour in my eyes, ask him to sign my book. I'll slip him my number on a piece of paper, wait for him as he leaves, take him home with me and wipe all those women from his memory, let him know they'll never love him like I love him, he'll never have a reader like me, his ideal reader. Here he comes… The event is beginning. I've been asked not to post on social media during the broadcast so as to maintain the illusion of a live stream. Perhaps I can slither into his DMs, something ambiguous and vaguely menacing. He's dressed in black (surprise) with a turtle-neck top: an outfit in quotation marks. His hair is greying – 'prematurely greying' as a journalist recently put it – but it suits him, for now at least. His interviewer is a woman who he hung out with a bit when he lived in Paris. She had moved there after a divorce or a break-up, was writing for a French newspaper. He remembers drinking with her in a wine bar near the Canal de l'Ourcq on a warm Sunday afternoon. She'd told him about a guy she seemed to have spent the night with, and he'd wondered whether something might happen between them. He recalls being a little intimidated by her moneyed air – some lingering class insecurity. He looks at ease now, playful, cracking lame jokes. What we know and the audience doesn't is that he used to find public appearances unnerving, having required therapy in his twenties to overcome a public-speaking phobia. During college, the phobia had triggered panic attacks that spiralled into a drug-exacerbated depression that swallowed up prime years of his life. What had made it frightening to stand up in front of crowds is that he compulsively projected himself into their minds, attributing to them perceptions as cruel and ruthless as those he trained on the world in those years. When he faced a crowd the adversary was out there, diffused, watching him with vicious attention, sensing his fear and weakness, knowing his secrets, his shame. On my screen he finishes reading from his book. I'm watching him carefully. After closing the book he tells the journalist that as far as he's concerned, all future literary festivals ought to be like this. Behind the woman is a primitivist painting of a naked woman in a forest or jungle, her breasts full and round. I sip coffee, reading the comments as they scroll alongside the video.

214

48 SAINT AUGUSTINE

Confessions (c. 400)

Translated by R.S. Pine-Coffin

Sixteen centuries after they were written, Saint Augustine's *Confessions* might induce in the secular reader a bout of faith-envy. The poignancy in Emil Cioran's observation hits home: 'Obviously God was a solution, and obviously none so satisfactory will ever be found again.'

A solution to what? To the problem of human life, of course. 'Have pity on me and heal me,' pleads Augustine of his God, 'For you see that I have become a problem to myself, and this is the ailment from which I suffer.' While Augustine's solution is a hard one for many of us landlocked here in modernity to pull off, the trials that inspired his *Confessions* are perennially relatable.

In his forties and a bishop in his native North Africa, Augustine recounts his licentious youth, his decade in thrall to the heretical creed of Manichaeism, and his eventual salvation through faith. Alternating between first- and an eroticised second-person, he disabuses contemporaries who might have assumed he was born impregnably pious. Raised by a Christian mother and a pagan father in what is now Algeria, the young Augustine harboured a devilish trait: he was very horny. They didn't have Tinder or Pornhub back then, yet the lad succumbed repeatedly to temptation, especially when he became a student: 'I went to Carthage, where I found myself in the midst of a hissing cauldron of lust.'

The prose (in Pine-Coffin's feisty translation) really flares up as Augustine lacerates himself for his sins and defilement. He may have renounced Jezebel, but there is a lingual lustiness in his castigation of a youth 'inflamed with desire for a surfeit of hell's pleasures'. He fornicates around, takes a mistress, blasphemes. At one point he either masturbates or has sex in a church. Much of *Confessions* details the skimmable fine print of his theological doubts before he finds blissful repose in God's love. Good for him; I just wish he'd gleaned a few more hot chapters from his years of depravity, when 'The evil in me was foul, but I loved it.'

A gay friend tells me that online you can find videos of virtually every male celebrity masturbating in front of his laptop, covertly recorded by hackers. It's not such a big deal any more, it seems; the celebrities get on with their careers and no one really makes a scandal. I find this reassuring, as I used to imagine that that would be the worst humiliation, to have an act of such intimacy made permanently visible to the whole world. Then again, although I work with prose and imagination rather than video, it strikes me that I've already posted the equivalent of numerous clips of me gratifying myself, and no one is going to take them down any time soon. Even when we read novelly novels we tend to see the narrator as the author, a person whom we can now observe and engage with on social media. I've already given my voyeur-readers plenty to work with, like a porn actress pouting from an array of thumbnails. I'm not entirely sure what's at the root of it, this seeming compulsion to publicly expose and debase myself in writing – violating my standards faster than I can lower them, as Robin Williams had it. The truth is, I'm more prudish than many. In an era of sex-positivity, I'm riddled with hang-ups, neuroses, tortured obsessions. My relationship to the feminine erotic archetype is, to use a Jungian term, completely fucked. I suspect that for writers who enjoy relatively uncomplicated, shame-free relationships to sexuality, it does not feature so prominently among their themes. And of course it is this very prudence on my part, this reticence, that accounts for the exhibitionistic and obsessive investigative drive. By plunging into indignity, swimming out beyond embarrassment and shame, I hope to discover what those in their easeful liberation seem to know – that it's all somehow fine, merely human, the fountain of life itself and not worth obsessing over.

49 JORGE LUIS BORGES

Fictions (1944)

Translated by Andrew Hurley

It's always worth reminding the general public that our time on earth is much enriched if we devote a bit of it to reading Jorge Luis Borges. Some suspect him of being icily cerebral (story titles like 'Tlön, Uqbar, Orbis Tertius' don't help), but really Borges is the most fun and accessible of modernists. And while he might warp or expand time, he'll never waste it: the short stories in *Fictions* are masterpieces of condensation. Borges impishly ascribed his preference for the short story to laziness, claiming it was too much bother to set out 'in five hundred pages an idea that can be perfectly related orally in five minutes'. Why not pretend that books – even whole literatures and civilisations – already exist, and provide commentaries on them instead?

Traditionally, short stories offer glimpses into human lives, charting emotional configurations and interpersonal disquiets. With the publication of *Fictions*, it was as if an alternate literary universe had been discovered in which none of our familiar laws applied. In stories like 'The Circular Ruins', 'Three Versions of Judas' and 'The Garden of Forking Paths', Borges smashed together philosophy, heretical theology, science fiction, detective thrillers, fantasy and hoax in his high-literary supercollider. Dreams within dreams, narrative hypercomplexity, glimpses of infinity: *Fictions* conjures up a sequence of inadvertent metaphors for the dizzying universe that contemporary physicists were beginning to uncover, as time and space proved spookier than we could have imagined.

The quantum comedy TV series *Rick and Morty* recently struck me as a vulgar pop cultural echo of the Borgesian Big Bang, with its head-spinning cosmological scenarios unfurled in twenty-minute jolts. Wasn't there even an episode in which Borges turned out to be a precocious teenager from a vastly advanced alien race, who came and revolutionised our primitive earth-literature just for kicks? Maybe not, but it's easy to see Borges's influence everywhere – not least because, in the literary century that followed him, it really is. Metafiction, postmodernism, even so-called autofiction: all of them are modulations on the Borgesian superstring. I'm calling it: he was his century's greatest writer.

When I was in the last spasms of prepubescence – emerging from that aforementioned latency period – I was reading not Jorge Luis Borges but Nick Hornby. Hornby was one of those rare literary novelists whose success penetrated even such proletarian households as I grew up in. Roddy Doyle also belongs to this category – in fact, he virtually invented it in Ireland, where mothers, fathers, grandparents, kids and everyone else got in on the action. Doyle's appeal lay in how he described working-class passions with irreverent comedy rather than piety, in prose of Bukowski-honed minimalism. Here were people who spoke the way we did, were anarchic and cheerfully profane like us, with the same pop-cultural references, living and loving in Dublin suburbs we clearly recognised but weren't used to seeing granted the status of literature. (Not that we ever talked about 'literature' in my family, beyond it being the word my dad used to denote promotional flyers and brochures.) In the case of Nick Hornby, the attraction was that of an articulate voice whose subject was again the stuff that interested people like us but which other writers ignored: football, basically. Everyone in my family read Fever Pitch *when it came out: a book about an Arsenal fan, like my two brothers (imitating my father, I followed Man United), and the unreasonable sway his fandom exerts on his emotional life. In that book, Hornby reflects on watching the Brazilian national team playing in the 1970 World Cup – a team so brilliant they effect a permanent shift in the collective football-watching consciousness:*

It wasn't just the quality of the football, though; it was the way they regarded ingenious and outrageous embellishment as though it were as functional and necessary as a corner kick or a throw-in. The only comparison I had at my disposal then was with toy cars: although I had no interest in Dinky or Corgi or Matchbox, I loved Lady Penelope's pink Rolls-Royce and James Bond's Aston Martin, both equipped with elaborate devices such as ejector seats and hidden guns which lifted them out of the boringly ordinary. Pelé's attempt to score from inside his own half with a lob, the dummy he sold to the Peruvian goalkeeper when he went one way round and the ball went the other... these were football's equivalent of the ejector seat, and made everything else look like so many Vauxhall Vivas.

This quality of 'outrageous and ingenious embellishment' is not far off what would attract me, a decade after reading Hornby, to Latin American literature, with Borges as its star player, running rings around everyone – a figure of such flair and novelty he seemed, like Pelé, more myth than human. I'd checked out a couple of Borges stories in college, after they kept getting referenced in Foucault and Baudrillard, but I didn't read him until somewhat later, when I was actually in Latin America – Buenos Aires, in fact. If we take this football analogy and dribble with it, what thrilled me so much in Latin American writing is that it was like a style of play that consisted solely of overhead kicks, dazzling swerves, miraculous feints and shimmies. In my twenties, I didn't really read the canonical American alpha novels of the twentieth century – your Roths and Updikes and Bellows. They looked to me too much like long-ball games, prudent 4–4–2 strategies, one-nil wins by stoic and sensible squads. Those books may well have been great but they seemed ordinary despite, or perhaps because of, this aura of established, stolid greatness. Latin American literature by contrast favoured play, kink, invention, flair, fancy footwork. There were novels whose author urged you to read the chapters in any order you liked; novels consisting entirely of footnotes; fictions fluent in the meta-trickery that excited me then, yet which didn't stint on atmospherics or thematic interest. When I read Borges's iconic volumes of 'fictions' (I liked that he didn't call them short stories, which would have been a concession to the literary mundane) in cafés in Argentina and Bolivia, his work effected the kind of massive cognitive 'download' – to use a word favoured by the ayahuascero future-hippies I met in the region – that reboots one's sense of literary possibility. (William Gibson likewise felt compelled to reach for a tech metaphor when describing the future-shock of encountering this writer born at the end of the nineteenth century: 'Had the concept of software been available to me, I imagine I would have felt as though I were installing something that exponentially increased what one day would be called bandwidth.') Borges invented a kind of fiction that skipped over the in-between stuff, the pages of filler you get through on the way to that flash of fascination. He was all tricks, all flair, all fascination. Borges was continuously trying to score from inside his own half or dummying the Peruvian goalkeeper – and not just trying, which would place him in that dismal category, the 'experimental writer', but succeeding. His work was proof of the existence of a hidden realm where every seat is an ejector seat, every car an Aston Martin with concealed guns, every footballer a Pelé or Maradona – a utopia out past convention, whose task it falls to each writer to discover for themselves.

The Death of Adam:
   Essays on Modern Thought (1998)

Marilynne Robinson belongs to a rare and attractive category of thinker: the contrarian of high moral seriousness. That is, her contrarianism stems not from congenital misanthropy, but from the union of a fertile system of values with an instinctual mistrust of consensus. I became interested in Robinson not through her much-loved novels, but through her recent essay collection *What Are We Doing Here?* Reading her felt faintly transgressive, in that one is not accustomed to modern intellectuals writing at full tilt from the starting point of an unabashed belief in God. When Robinson writes about religion, it really does seem a more coherent stance towards existence than whatever is meant by atheism: religion has 'its origins in the human intuition that reality is rooted in a profounder matrix of Being than sense and experience make known to us in the ordinary course of things. By theology I mean the attempts to realise in some degree the vastness and atmospheres of this matrix of Being.'

Robinson's earlier collection, *The Death of Adam*, reappraises certain historical figures and schools of thought around whom our views are so cosily consensual that we have long ceased thinking about them, 'a campaign of revisionism, because contemporary discourse feels to me empty and false'. What could be more countercultural than a spirited bid to rehabilitate John Calvin, that scarecrow-signifier of religious gloom and Christian self-hatred? 'My heart is with the Puritans,' Robinson admits with an air of lofty mischief, while taking pains to distinguish the genuine, self-effacing morality she admires from mere priggishness ('signs by which they make themselves recognisable to others and to themselves as virtuous').

Decrying the societal and ecological carcinogen of free-market economics, Robinson traces the brutal anti-values underpinning them to the more or less explicit calls to exterminate the weak found in Nietzsche and Darwin. Occasionally she comes close to denouncing the entire project of modern thought itself. In going after such big game, an author could make herself ridiculous; Robinson's patent sanity and earthed, life-loving conservatism make me trust her.

Throughout this book, by way of the novelists and philosophers I've endorsed, it strikes me that I've been acting tough, playing the punk, not missing an opportunity to let you know how hard-boiled and comfortless my world view has become. I talk a big game, but the truth is that long before reading Freud, Nietzsche and the splenetic malcontents recruited here, I was a good Catholic boy. Throughout childhood I went to mass every Sunday, prayed at night, knelt in the dark of the confessional one Saturday morning a month. I feared hell, crossed myself whenever an ambulance passed, hoped for heaven and assumed that's where I was going. Then came puberty, punk, alcohol, drugs, wayward books, the fascination of evil. My boyhood devoutness fell away. Or so I thought until, a decade or so down the line, I underwent the commonplace realisation that the creed which shapes you runs deeper than any nominal repudiation can uproot. It dawns on you that your destiny on the earth is that of a being divided, pulled between the old world and the one that's drawing us towards the horizon, not fully at home in either. In short, it hits you that in your bones and cells you're a Christian, a Catholic, regardless of what you've told yourself or others you believe. It's not even about anything so binary and literal as belief in a God; it's about prejudice, outlook, the cast of your afflictions. And what are the marks, the stigmata of this phantom Christianity that groans under the floorboards? Well, for one thing, your relationship to sex will always be fundamentally dark, uneasy, lacking in lightness or innocence; it is not, shall we say, Mediterranean. Sexuality plays out within you as an inherited trauma. It is not separable from cruelty, harm, panic. More embarrassing still, you find in your core evidence of a humiliating cliché, a backward notion that you and everyone else really thought we'd have gotten over by now. It's in your attitude to women, in whom you've never been able to reconcile the coexistence of a carnal, desiring, appetiteful body – just as selfish and heedless as your own – alongside that of a nurturing, kindly, gracious spirit. The virgin and the whore! You act all modern and you screw around, take what you can get, but in your mangled heart you don't want female sexuality to be liberated; or you want it to be but only in your direction. All women have a priori betrayed you. They can never live up. They are not your devoted concubines or adoring slaves, therefore your relationship to them will forever lurch between tenderness and revulsion, desire and disappointment. Your attitude towards women as a collective will be tainted by fear, essentially adversarial. All of these are tormenting yet fertile contradictions, so you may as well become an artist. Meanwhile, the world being what it is, you must under no circumstances give voice to these awkward truths – not in the workplace, not online, not in books – because they are pariah attitudes, disdained by the crowd and by you too. You come to understand something of how it must feel to be a paedophile, racked by deplorable impulses you didn't choose and can't seem to uproot. And so you begin to go underground and live a double life, smiling up here on the surface, in daylight; but, down below, squinting and panting in the dingy cellar of the self, under busy streets from where you can hear the sound of footsteps and laughter, fascinated and appalled to realise that you're a monster.

51 ALBERT CAMUS

The Fall (1956)

Translated by Robin Buss

Rereading the last novel Albert Camus published in his life-time, I am left with two thoughts: first, that it's still excellent, and second, that I'm glad I encountered it when I did, namely during adolescence. It's hard to imagine *The Fall* having the impact on someone in their thirties that it can on a teenager. Regarded from the twenty-first century, existentialism itself, with its trench-coated, smoke-veiled fixation on cosmic indifference, seems like the troubled adolescence of human-kind: it was a phase we were going through. As a novelist, Camus was an ideas man, and the main idea driving *The Fall* – that altruism is covert self-gratification, while charm, social success, and sexual conquest belie a will to absolute dominion – stops feeling like news around age twenty.

The Fall is set in Amsterdam, whose concentric canals remind the cultivated, loquacious, forty-year-old narrator, Jean-Baptiste Clamence, of the circles of hell. In a seedy sailors' bar, he recounts his story to an unseen listener: how he attained a pinnacle of worldly success as a well-known lawyer in Paris, admiring his reflection in the gratitude of downtrodden clients whom he served pro bono, not to mention in the submissive bodies and adoring smiles of the women he collected like medals. After a sinister confrontation with his own cowardice on the banks of the Seine, how-ever, Clamence's glowing self-appraisal begins to crumble: a strange disembodied laughter pursues him through the Paris streets. And so it is that he winds up in a dim Amsterdam bar, recasting himself as a 'judge-penitent' who seduces unsuspecting listeners with his self-damning monologue, but only to force an equally nasty self-confrontation in the other, thereby affirming his own dominance.

Camus undoubtedly put a lot of himself into Jean-Baptiste Clamence – his glory, his supreme self-confidence, his attractiveness. Clamence's epigrammatic discourse on the despotic psychology of the womaniser is thus extra disquieting: 'I loved women – which amounts to saying that I never loved any one of them.'

Is there a book you wish you'd read at a younger age? A book you wish you'd never read? Which book damaged you the most? Which novel did you give to girls, or to guys, to help them understand you? Did you steal any books? Which ones? Which book did you give up reading with sixty pages to go and thereafter always regret not finishing (knowing it was somehow too late)? Which novel did you leave on a train and never learn how it turned out? Have you fallen in love with, or had a crush on, a fictional character? Been sexually aroused by reading? Have you gotten yourself off to a book? Is there an author you found yourself thinking more about than you did any person in your real life? How much about a novel can you remember after you've read it? Was Schopenhauer right when he claimed we remember our lives only a little better than a novel we once read? How well do you remember? Which scene do you wish you could forget? Which chapter would you most like to reread? When you get to the last page will you want to turn back to the start and read it again, or will you be relieved that it's over? Were there parts you skimmed? Were you left with more questions than answers? Did it cohere, or did it feel like a bundle of scenes flung haphazardly together? Was there a point where you felt the author lost his way? Was the prose refined or coarse, spare or ornate? Was it explicit and shocking? Did it make you laugh out loud much? Were the characters sympathetic, and were there any you would describe as evil? How accessible was it? What was the narrator like? What was the genre?

*Was it too long, too short, about the right length? Would
you read another of the author's works? Would you give it a
positive review?*

The Colossus of Maroussi (1941)

How can we escape the gloom and dejection that dominate modern literature? Why, by reading Henry Miller of course! We are told that happiness writes white and perhaps it does, but in Miller's case it's a supernal, brilliant white and I could use more of it. As the Second World War erupted, pushing fifty and fancying a break after two decades of writing, Miller travelled to Greece to visit his young friend Lawrence Durrell. The luminous, blissful book that resulted from his transformative time there was Miller's favourite of his own works and it may be mine too.

I've never read a book with so much light in it, wherein dazzle and radiance become theme and narrative. The light 'is not the light of the Mediterranean alone, it is something more, something unfathomable, something holy'. *The Colossus of Maroussi* is a travelogue penned when the planet still was lonely, or at least not yet black with Instagrammers, and the wanderer could encounter a place virginally so that it might even inspire a spiritual rebirth. The landscapes that overwhelm Miller's senses are ultimately emotional and metaphysical. His vision of Greece is generous to the point of sentimentalism, but he idealises it so as to denounce by contrast the sick American way of life he could see debasing the world in its own image. ('I can't stand this idea, which is rooted in the minds of little peoples, that America is the hope of the world.')

Miller had an Olympian sense of himself, but in its sweetness and light *Maroussi* bears less of the mystic-surrealist bombast to which he was prone. He liked himself a great deal, and persuades us to like him too – we want to keep travelling, drinking, swimming, laughing in his company. After a climactic visit to an ego-boosting Armenian soothsayer in Athens, Miller determines that he will transcend the art that was only ever training for his true masterpiece: life. *Maroussi* is his ode to joy and panegyric to generosity: from here on in he would use his immense, Whitmanian self for good.

BERLIN, 2019

Miller wrote a book titled The Books in My Life. *I haven't read it, but that's a good title, an honest title. And that's what* this *book has been: some of the books in my life, and some of the life too – the life in my books. One day I might write another book composed not of memories and literature but purely of colours, because right now that's what I'd like to convey: the colours. Specifically, the colours of the sea and the sky out here where I've walked each day while composing these dreams and reflections, waiting for the planet to wake from its strange sleep. The drinkable blues; the lazuli and indigo and all those hues whose names I never knew; the turquoise sparkle on a calm sea; the frothing whites trailed by ferries bound for distant ports; the violet evenings, which are now the long evenings of incipient summer. I envy painters, who are not obligated to narrate but need simply compose a mood from light and shade. The only colours I get to work with are white and black (if they even are colours), and so as compensation I write about wandering and journeys, that being the closest I can get to the simplicity and sensuousness of painting. I* must *be a frustrated painter, because I'm writing this final page* en plein air. *Rather than finish the book while propped against a pile of pillows in bed, I've walked out along the cliffs, to the headland at the curve of the coast, and clambered down onto the beach. It's deep blue and golden, the finest day of a fine early May. I have the vista to myself. More accurately, I share it with the seabirds perched on the jawline of rock just offshore, and the seals that bob in the waves near where I've laid my mat. I needed to leave the screens at home, my umbilical cord to a cabin-feverish globe. Tuskar Rock lighthouse is out there on the horizon, a white erection, site of many sunken ships and an airline flight that went down and left no survivors. But let's not think about death and loss, because this is a place where I feel at peace. A few years ago I used to come out here while microdosing on LSD, spend hours wiggling my toes in the sand. A frivolous way to pass one's time on earth, no doubt, but I was happy enough. After I write these sentences I'll lie down and close my eyes, the breeze on my skin, the surge of waves in my ear. I'll drift off and dream of lives on the other shore, friendly greetings, an exotic tongue, laughing children. I think I've dozed off already and am dreaming this page. I dedicate it to the seals, who care little for a system in peril, an uncertain future. May they inherit the earth. Their skin is slippery and dappled with sunlight as they curl and dive in the surf, like cosmic dancers. I think I'll join them soon, run with their crew, plumb the depths. It was fun to wear a human suit a while, play that funny role. Now it's time to bow out with grace, let the fauna run things for an epoch, check our privilege. Salutations, frolicking seals, I will meet you on the other shore.*

ROSSLARE HARBOUR, 2020

ACKNOWLEDGEMENTS

My thanks first of all to Martin Doyle for giving me the opportunity to write the *Irish Times* column that became the basis for this book. Warm thanks to Joseph O'Connor, Sarah Moore-Fitzgerald, Donal Ryan, and all my colleagues and students at the University of Limerick, under whose auspices I wrote *Autobibliography* as the inaugural Kate O'Brien PhD Fellow in Creative Writing – their support was generous, indulgent and unstinting. Thanks to Andy West, Simon Kelly, Phil Kelly and Simon Brennan for reading and commenting on the individual columns before they were published, even if they didn't always ask for the privilege, such being the magic of private messaging groups. Thanks to Mark Richards for so enthusiastically getting behind this book, and to Alex Billington and Seán Costello for carefully overseeing its production and fine-tuning. I'm grateful to Antony Farrell for suggesting I expand my newspaper column into a book, and to my agent Sam Copeland. Special thanks to Roisin Kiberd for the infinite conversation, the warm vaporwave nights by the beach, and the vital help in myriad forms. Finally, thanks as ever to my family and all my friends.